Carson McCullers

The Ballad of the Sad Café

Text and Study Aids

Edited and annotated
by Tobias Hergt

Ernst Klett Verlag

ISBN 3-12-578900-1

1. Auflage 1 6 5 4 | 1989 88 87

Alle Drucke dieser Auflage können im Unterricht nebeneinander benutzt werden, sie sind untereinander unverändert. Die letzte Zahl bezeichnet das Jahr dieses Druckes.

Umschlaggestaltung: Hans Lämmle, Stuttgart.
Druck: Wilhelm Röck, Weinsberg. Printed in Germany.

Contents

Carson McCullers and the South

The region of the South – stretching from Baltimore to New Orleans – includes the present states of Maryland, Virginia, West Virginia, North Carolina, South Carolina, Georgia, Kentucky, Tennessee, Louisiana, Mississippi, Alabama, Missouri, Arkansas, Florida and Eastern Texas. Parts of the area were colonized by the French and Spanish during and after the 16th century. Jamestown, Virginia, was the first permanent English settlement on American soil (1607). From the beginning, the South was almost exclusively agrarian, and in the course of time an aristocracy of plantation owners came into being which formed a leisure class dedicated to educational goals and intellectual activities. Thus, education tended to be restricted to the upper classes.

During the 19th century the economic system of the South, based on agriculture and the slave trade, separated the region from the increasingly industrialized North. Feelings of rivalry and animosity reached their peak in the Civil War (1861-65) when the South tried to achieve independence from the North by forming a Confederacy. In the post-war period, known as Reconstruction, during which the South was virtually an occupied country, the former social and economic framework was changed through the abolition of slavery and the new status of the Negroes, even though attitudes of discrimination and segregation remained and were consciously perpetuated. The Ku Klux Klan tried to counteract the influence of Northern ideology in the South by keeping the Negro population in constant fear of their terrorist activities. After the Civil War, authors used the setting of the pre-war South as a subject of literary imagination, but many of them glorified the ante-bellum South, trying to recreate the past rather than comment critically on the present.

In the 20s and 30s of this century the literature of the South gained so much momentum and developed such a marked sense of its own identity that literary historians spoke of a Southern Literary Renascence. Prominent modern writers of the South are William Faulkner (the most prominent of all), Thomas Wolfe, John Crowe Ransom, Allen Tate, Katherine Anne Porter, Erskine Caldwell, Robert Penn Warren, Caroline Gordon, Carson McCullers, Eudora

Welty, Flannery O'Connor, Truman Capote, William Styron, Cormack McCarthy and James Dicky. Tendencies toward uniformity and standardization of life in the South, however, make the future perspectives of a genuinely Southern fiction that is original and creative in its scope seem not too promising. Some literary critics therefore speak of a decline in, or even the death of, Southern fiction.

Carson McCullers (née Smith) was born on February 19, 1917, in the small town of Columbus, Georgia, a town some 80 miles southwest of Atlanta. Her father was an industrious jeweller and watch repairman, her mother, of Irish descent, took care of Carson and her younger brother and sister. Her family was part of the small-town middle class. The mother instilled in Carson an early feeling of importance and ingenuity. Thus, even as a young girl, Carson developed a strong sense of her own brilliancy and – with passion and discipline – always did her best to prove her talents. This driving impulse put some strain on her relationship with other children as well as with adults.

She played the piano very well, furthering her skills by a severe daily programme of practice. It is not surprising therefore that until the age of 15 she thought she would enter on the career of a concert pianist and, after high school graduation in 1933, planned to attend the well-known Juilliard School of Music in New York City. At the same time, however, an up to then dormant interest in literature awoke in her, so that she started reading profusely, concentrating on Greek philosophy and drama, Russian, German, and French literature in translation, and "masterpieces" of British and American writing. She made her own attempts at Creative Writing, composing two plays (imitations of O'Neill's) and a few short stories ("Wunderkind") that reflected her adolescent experience.

At age 17, Carson travelled to New York City where she worked at odd jobs and studied Creative Writing at Columbia and New York Universities. Three years later she married Reeves McCullers, a corporal in the army, whom she had been friends with for some years. They first lived in North Carolina where Reeves got a job in a credit corporation while Carson was finishing work on her first novel, *The Heart Is a Lonely Hunter,* which was published in 1940. Its central character is a deaf-mute Jew in a small Georgia mill town whose quiet smile and perpetual silence give an impression of wisdom and compassion. He gains the confidence of six individuals who lack an audience for their views and confessions. Carson McCullers immediately won great recognition for her novel. Her outstanding success encouraged Reeves and Carson to move North to New York and take quarters in Greenwich Village, the artists' district, where they met internationally-known Anglo-American and foreign writers, critics, artists, among them exiles from Nazi Germany, like Klaus and Erika Mann, Kantorowicz, etc. This move North was the beginning of a constant shuttling back and forth between her home town of Columbus, where she joined her family and relaxed, and the North, where she mainly did her creative work.

The marriage between Reeves and Carson failed because of personality clashes, mutual egotism, disappointments. Reeves, who also strongly wished to become a writer, had wanted to take turns with his wife in their periods of creative activity, but soon realized that he would always be the one who had to keep their household organized and support her in her more and more complicated ailments. She suffered her first stroke at age 23 and throughout her life was plagued by various severe illnesses. Carson, on the other hand, was fascinated by the intellectual and artistic experience and the social opportunities that her startling success as a young novelist offered her. So quite frequently she felt tied up and restricted by the union with her husband. She attended writers' conferences and took advantage of scholarships and grants that enabled her to work in artists' colonies, thereby getting more and more involved in the contemporary literary scene and being able to exchange ideas and gain inspiration. Her life as a sensitive artist estranged her from her husband. She initiated divorce proceedings which were finalized in 1941. That year her second novel, *Reflections in a Golden Eye,* was published, in addition to a few essays on the war in Europe.

After seeing her former husband several times between 1943 and 1945 the two decided to remarry. Reeves had served overseas after re-entering the army and had participated in three major campaigns in the final struggle between the Allies and Nazi Germany. He had been promoted to captain but was discharged for physical disability. In the meantime, Carson had been able to sustain her artistic productivity despite constant and increasingly threatening illnesses that were no doubt aggravated by chain-smoking and alcohol. In 1943, *The Ballad of the Sad Café* was published in *Harper's Bazaar;* three years later Houghton Mifflin published *The Member of the Wedding,* a second short novel describing the process of growing up of a girl named Frankie Addams. Like so many of Carson McCullers' works, *The Member of the Wedding* deals with human loneliness. Frankie Addams thinks of her brother and his bride as the "*we* of me": "For a long time now her brother and the bride had been at Winter Hill. They had left the town a hundred miles behind them, and now were in a city far away. They were them and in Winter Hill, together, while she was her and in the same old town all by herself. The long hundred miles did not make her sadder and make her feel more far away than the knowing that they were them and both together and she was only her and parted from them, by herself. And as she sickened with this feeling a thought and explanation suddenly came to her, so that she knew and almost said aloud: *They are the we of me*. Yesterday, and all the twelve years of her life, she had only been Frankie. She was an *I* person who had to walk around and do things by herself. All other people had a *we* to claim, all other except her."

Mrs. McCullers used the money from a second Guggenheim Fellowship to travel to Europe together with her husband. They visited Paris, and she met major Italian writers in Rome.

In 1949/50 the dramatized version of *The Member of the Wedding,* which Carson had worked out in Tennessee Williams' Nantucket home, was produced in Philadelphia and New York. The production met with enthusiastic praise and paid off financially. In Europe, the play was successful, too. Several more trips to Europe were to follow, on one of which Reeves McCullers committed suicide.

Mrs. McCullers' play *The Square Root of Wonderful* (1957) proved a failure as far as public esteem was concerned, which deeply depressed the playwright. It did not discourage her, however, from working on yet another novel, *Clock without Hands,* which was published in 1961. She also wrote a few poems, published posthumously in *The Mortgaged Heart*.

In August 1967 Carson McCullers suffered a final stroke, a massive brain hemorrhage, and remained in a state of unconsciousness until she died in November in a New York hospital at the age of 50.

The Ballad of the Sad Café

I The town itself is dreary; not much is there except the cotton mill, the two-room houses where the workers live, a few peach trees, a church with two colored windows, and a miserable main street only a hundred yards long. On Saturdays the tenants from the near-by farms come in for a day of talk and trade. Otherwise the town is lonesome, sad, and like a place that is far off and estranged from all other places in the world. The nearest train stop is Society City, and the Greyhound and White Bus Lines use the Forks Falls Road which is three miles away. The winters here are short and raw, the summers white with glare and fiery hot.

If you walk along the main street on an August afternoon there is nothing whatsoever to do. The largest building, in the very center of the town, is boarded up completely and leans so far to the right that it seems bound to collapse at any minute. The house is very old. There is about it a curious, cracked look that is very puzzling until you suddenly realize that at one time, and long ago, the right side of the front porch had been painted, and part of the wall – but the painting was left unfinished and one portion of the house is darker and dingier than the other. The building looks completely deserted. Nevertheless, on the second floor there is one window which is not boarded; sometimes in the late afternoon when the heat is at its worst a hand will slowly open the shutter and a face will look down on the town. It is a face like the terrible dim faces known in dreams – sexless and white, with two gray crossed eyes which are turned inward so sharply that they seem to be exchanging with each other one long and

dreary ['drɪərɪ] gloomy; causing low spirits (traurig) – *cotton mill* factory in which cloth is manufactured from cotton (Baumwollspinnerei) – *tenant* ['– –] person who pays rent for the use of land (Pächter) – *estranged from* apart from – *raw* (here) cold and damp – *glare* strong, fierce, unpleasant light – *dingy* ['dɪndʒɪ] dirty and faded – *to desert* [dɪ'zɜ:t] to leave empty

secret gaze of grief. The face lingers at the window for an hour or so, then the shutters are closed once more, and as likely as not there will not be another soul to be seen along the main street. These August afternoons – when your shift is finished there is absolutely nothing to do; you might as well walk down to the Forks Falls Road and listen to the chain gang.

However, here in this very town there was once a café. And this old boarded-up house was unlike any other place for many miles around. There were tables with cloths and paper napkins, colored streamers from the electric fans, great gatherings on Saturday nights. The owner of the place was Miss Amelia Evans. But the person most responsible for the success and gaiety of the place was a hunchback called Cousin Lymon. One other person had a part in the story of this café – he was the former husband of Miss Amelia, a terrible character who returned to the town after a long term in the penitentiary, caused ruin, and then went on his way again. The café has long since been closed, but it is still remembered.

II The place was not always a café. Miss Amelia inherited the building from her father, and it was a store that carried mostly feed, guano, and staples such as meal and snuff. Miss Amelia was rich. In addition to the store she operated a still three miles back in the swamp, and ran out the best liquor in the county. She was a dark, tall woman with bones and muscles like a man. Her hair was cut short and brushed back from the forehead, and there was about her sunburned face a tense, haggard quality. She might have been a handsome woman if, even then, she was not slightly cross-eyed. There were those who would have courted her, but Miss Amelia cared

to linger to be slow to disappear – *as likely as not* most probably – *chain gang* ['– –] a group of prisoners chained together for work outside their prison – *napkin* piece of paper or cloth used when eating to clean hands and lips – *streamer* long narrow piece of coloured paper – *hunchback* a person with a back misshaped by a round hump (Buckliger) – *penitentiary* [penɪ'tenʃərɪ] prison – *staple* chief product of a country or district – *still* distillery; an establishment where alcoholic liquors are distilled – *swamp* an area of soft wet land (Moor) – *to run out* (here) to sell – *haggard* ['hægəd] having a wasted and worn look, as from sleeplessness and grief

nothing for the love of men and was a solitary person. Her marriage had been unlike any other marriage ever contracted in this county – it was a strange and dangerous marriage, lasting only for ten days, that left the whole town wondering and shocked. Except for this queer marriage, Miss Amelia had lived her life alone. Often she spent whole nights back in her shed in the swamp, dressed in overalls and gum boots, silently guarding the low fire of the still.

With all things which could be made by the hands Miss Amelia prospered. She sold chitterlins and sausage in the town near-by. On fine autumn days, she ground sorghum, and the syrup from her vats was dark golden and delicately flavored. She built the brick privy behind her store in only two weeks and was skilled in carpentering. It was only with people that Miss Amelia was not at ease. People, unless they are nilly-willy or very sick, cannot be taken into the hands and changed overnight to something more worthwhile and profitable. So that the only use that Miss Amelia had for other people was to make money out of them. And in this she succeeded. Mortgages on crops and property, a sawmill, money in the bank – she was the richest woman for miles around. She would have been rich as a congressman if it were not for her one great failing, and that was her passion for lawsuits and the courts. She would involve herself in long and bitter litigation over just a trifle. It was said that if Miss Amelia so much as stumbled over a rock in the road she would glance around instinctively as though looking for something to sue about it. Aside from these lawsuits she lived a steady life and every day was very

solitary alone; without companions – *to prosper* to become successful and rich – *chitterlins* (dial.) the small intestines of pigs, used for food (Kutteln, Innereien vom Schwein) – *sorghum* a type of corn grown in warm areas; a thick sweet syrup made from this – *vat* large container for holding liquids – *privy* ['prɪvɪ] toilet without a water supply – *willy-nilly* of very weak character – *mortgage* ['mɔːgɪdʒ] an agreement to have money lent, esp. so as to buy a house, with the house or land belonging to the lender until the money is repaid (Hypothek) – *sawmill* – place where wood is sawn by machinery – *lawsuit* request made to a court of law to get s.th. back or to be paid for damage suffered – *litigation* process of carrying on a lawsuit in court – *trifle* ['traɪfəl] a thing of little value or importance – *to sue* to bring a claim in law against, esp. for an amount of money

much like the day that had gone before. With the exception of her ten-day marriage, nothing happened to change this until the spring of the year that Miss Amelia was thirty years old.

It was toward midnight on a soft quiet evening in April. The sky was the color of a blue swamp iris, the moon clear and bright. The crops that spring promised well and in the past weeks the mill had run a night shift. Down by the creek the square brick factory was yellow with light, and there was the faint, steady hum of the looms. It was such a night when it is good to hear from faraway, across the dark fields, the slow song of a Negro on his way to make love. Or when it is pleasant to sit quietly and pick a guitar, or simply to rest alone and think of nothing at all. The street that evening was deserted, but Miss Amelia's store was lighted and on the porch outside there were five people. One of these was Stumpy MacPhail, a foreman with a red face and dainty, purplish hands. On the top step were two boys in overalls, the Rainey twins – both of them lanky and slow, with white hair and sleepy green eyes. The other man was Henry Macy, a shy and timid person with gentle manners and nervous ways, who sat on the edge of the bottom step. Miss Amelia herself stood leaning against the side of the open door, her feet crossed in their big swamp boots, patiently untying knots in a rope she had come across. They had not talked for a long time.

One of the twins, who had been looking down the empty road, was the first to speak. "I see something coming," he said.

"A calf got loose," said his brother.

The approaching figure was still too distant to be clearly seen. The moon made dim, twisted shadows of the blossoming peach trees along the side of the road. In the air the odor of blossoms and sweet

iris ['aɪərɪs] tall yellow or purple and white flower with large leaves – *crop* a plant such as grain, fruit, or vegetables grown by a farmer (Getreide, Ernte) – *shift* a group of workers which takes turns with one or more other groups (Schicht) – *loom* machine on which thread is woven into cloth (Webstuhl) – *dainty* small, pretty, clean, and delicate – *lanky* very thin and ungracefully tall or long – *timid* fearful; lacking courage – *to untie* to undo a knot or s.th. tied – *to twist* to wind or turn one thing round another – *to blossom* to produce flowers – *odor* smell

spring grass mingled with the warm, sour smell of the near-by lagoon.

"No. It's somebody's youngun," said Stumpy MacPhail.

Miss Amelia watched the road in silence. She had put down her rope and was fingering the straps of her overalls with her brown bony hand. She scowled, and a dark lock of hair fell down on her forehead. While they were waiting there, a dog from one of the houses down the road began a wild, hoarse howl that continued until a voice called out and hushed him. It was not until the figure was quite close, within the range of the yellow light from the porch, that they saw clearly what had come.

The man was a stranger, and it is rare that a stranger enters the town on foot at that hour. Besides, the man was a hunchback. He was scarcely more than four feet tall and he wore a ragged, dusty coat that reached only to his knees. His crooked little legs seemed too thin to carry the weight of his great warped chest and the hump that sat on his shoulders. He had a very large head, with deep-set blue eyes and a sharp little mouth. His face was both soft and sassy – at the moment his pale skin was yellowed by dust and there were lavender shadows beneath his eyes. He carried a lopsided old suitcase which was tied with a rope.

"Evening," said the hunchback, and he was out of breath.

Miss Amelia and the men on the porch neither answered his greeting nor spoke. They only looked at him.

"I am hunting for Miss Amelia Evans."

Miss Amelia pushed back her hair from her forehead and raised her chin. "How come?"

"Because I am kin to her," the hunchback said.

lagoon [lə'gu:n] a lake of sea water separated from the sea – *youngun* (sl.) young one, child – *to scowl* [skaʊl] to give one's face an angry, threatening expression – *hoarse* rough and harsh-sounding – *to hush* to cause to be silent – *range* [reɪndʒ] the distance at which one can see or hear – *porch* a built-out, roofed entrance to a house; veranda – *ragged* ['rægɪd] old and torn – *crooked* ['krʊkɪd] not straight; twisted; dishonest – *warped* turned or twisted out of shape – *hump* a round part which stands out noticeably – *sassy* cheeky, bold – *lavender* ['lævəndə] a plant with strongly-smelling purple flowers (Lavendel) – *lopsided* not balanced – *to be kin to* to be a relative of

The twins and Stumpy MacPhail looked up at Miss Amelia.

"That's me," she said. "How do you mean 'kin'?"

"Because – –" the hunchback began. He looked uneasy, almost as though he was about to cry. He rested the suitcase on the bottom step, but did not take his hand from the handle. "My mother was Fanny Jesup and she come from Cheehaw. She left Cheehaw some thirty years ago when she married her first husband. I remember hearing her tell how she had a half-sister named Martha. And back in Cheehaw today they tell me that was your mother."

Miss Amelia listened with her head turned slightly aside. She ate her Sunday dinners by herself; her place was never crowded with a flock of relatives, and she claimed kin with no one. She had had a great-aunt who owned the livery stable in Cheehaw, but that aunt was now dead. Aside from her there was only one double first cousin who lived in a town twenty miles away, but this cousin and Miss Amelia did not get on so well, and when they chanced to pass each other they spat on the side of the road. Other people had tried very hard, from time to time, to work out some kind of far-fetched connection with Miss Amelia, but with absolutely no success.

The hunchback went into a long rigmarole, mentioning names and places that were unknown to the listeners on the porch and seemed to have nothing to do with the subject. "So Fanny and Martha Jesup were half-sisters. And I am the son of Fanny's third husband. So that would make you and I – –" He bent down and began to unfasten his suitcase. His hands were like dirty sparrow claws and they were trembling. The bag was full of all manner of junk – ragged clothes and odd rubbish that looked like parts out of a sewing machine, or something just as worthless. The hunchback scrambled among these belongings and brought out an old photograph. "This is a picture of my mother and her half-sister."

Miss Amelia did not speak. She was moving her jaw slowly from side to side, and you could tell from her face what she was thinking

livery stable a place where owners may pay to have their horses kept and fed – *rigmarole* a long confused story without much meaning – *sparrow* small brownish bird common in many parts of the world – *junk* old useless things – *to scramble* to move quickly over a rough surface – *jaw* one of the two bony parts of the face in which the teeth are set (Kiefer)

about. Stumpy MacPhail took the photograph and held it out toward the light. It was a picture of two pale, withered-up little children of about two and three years of age. The faces were tiny white blurs, and it might have been an old picture in anyone's album.

Stumpy MacPhail handed it back with no comment. "Where you come from?" he asked.

The hunchback's voice was uncertain. "I was traveling."

Still Miss Amelia did not speak. She just stood leaning against the side of the door, and looked down at the hunchback. Henry Macy winked nervously and rubbed his hands together. Then quietly he left the bottom step and disappeared. He is a good soul, and the hunchback's situation had touched his heart. Therefore he did not want to wait and watch Miss Amelia chase this newcomer off her property and run him out of town. The hunchback stood with his bag open on the bottom step; he sniffled his nose, and his mouth quivered. Perhaps he began to feel his dismal predicament. Maybe he realized what a miserable thing it was to be a stranger in the town with a suitcase full of junk, and claiming kin with Miss Amelia. At any rate he sat down on the steps and suddenly began to cry.

It was not a common thing to have an unknown hunchback walk to the store at midnight and then sit down and cry. Miss Amelia rubbed back her hair from her forehead and the men looked at each other uncomfortably. All around the town was very quiet.

At last one of the twins said: "I'll be damned if he ain't a regular Morris Finestein."

Everyone nodded and agreed, for that is an expression having a certain special meaning. But the hunchback cried louder because he could not know what they were talking about. Morris Finestein was a person who had lived in the town years before. He was only a quick, skipping little Jew who cried if you called him Christ-killer,

withered-up reduced in size – *blur* s.th. whose shape is not clearly seen – *to wink* to close and open one eye rapidly – *to chase* to cause to leave – *to sniffle* to draw air into the nose with a sound in order to keep liquid from running out of the nose (schniefen) – *to quiver* to tremble a little – *predicament* [prɪ'dɪkəmənt] a difficult situation in which one does not know what to do – *to skip* to move in a light dancing way

and ate light bread and canned salmon every day. A calamity had come over him and he had moved away to Society City. But since then if a man were prissy in any way, or if a man ever wept, he was known as a Morris Finestein.

"Well, he is afflicted," said Stumpy MacPhail. "There is some cause."

Miss Amelia crossed the porch with two slow, gangling strides. She went down the steps and stood looking thoughtfully at the stranger. Gingerly, with one long brown forefinger, she touched the hump on his back. The hunchback still wept, but he was quieter now. The night was silent and the moon still shone with a soft, clear light – it was getting colder. Then Miss Amelia did a rare thing; she pulled out a bottle from her hip pocket and after polishing off the top with the palm of her hand she handed it to the hunchback to drink. Miss Amelia could seldom be persuaded to sell her liquor on credit, and for her to give so much as a drop away free was almost unknown.

"Drink," she said. "It will liven your gizzard."

The hunchback stopped crying, neatly licked the tears from around his mouth, and did as he was told. When he was finished, Miss Amelia took a slow swallow, warmed and washed her mouth with it, and spat. Then she also drank. The twins and the foreman had their own bottle they had paid for.

"It is smooth liquor," Stumpy MacPhail said. "Miss Amelia, I have never known you to fail."

The whisky they drank that evening (two big bottles of it) is important. Otherwise, it would be hard to account for what followed. Perhaps without it there would never have been a café. For the liquor of Miss Amelia has a special quality of its own. It is clean

salmon ['sæmən] large fish of the northern oceans with silvery skin (Lachs) – *calamity* a terrible event – *prissy* very precise; fussy (zimperlich) – *afflicted* suffering in the body or mind – *gangling* awkward – *stride* a long step when walking – *gingerly* ['dʒɪndʒəlɪ] in a way that is careful and controlled in movement so as not to cause harm – *hip* the fleshy part of either side of the human body above the legs – *to liven* ['laɪvən] to cause to become lively – *gizzard* ['gɪzəd] (humorous) stomach – *swallow* act of moving food down the throat – *smooth* [smu:ð] pleasant in the mouth and sharp on the tongue, but once down a man it glows inside him for a long time afterward. And that is not all. It is known that if a message is written with lemon juice on a clean sheet of paper there will be no sign of it. But if the paper is held for a moment to the fire then the letters turn brown and the meaning becomes clear. Imagine that the whisky is the fire and that the message is that which is known only in the soul of a man – then the worth of Miss Amelia's liquor can be understood. Things that have gone unnoticed, thoughts that have been harbored far back in the dark mind, are suddenly recognized and comprehended. A spinner who has thought only of the loom, the dinner pail, the bed, and then the loom again – this spinner might drink some on a Sunday and come across a marsh lily. And in his palm he might hold this flower, examining the golden dainty cup, and in him suddenly might come a sweetness keen as pain. A weaver might look up suddenly and see for the first time the cold, weird radiance of midnight January sky, and a deep fright at his own smallness stop his heart. Such things as these, then, happen when a man has drunk Miss Amelia's liquor. He may suffer, or he may be spent with joy – but the experience has shown the truth; he has warmed his soul and seen the message hidden there.

III They drank until it was past midnight, and the moon was clouded over so that the night was cold and dark. The hunchback still sat on the bottom steps, bent over miserably with his forehead resting on his knee. Miss Amelia stood with her hands in her pockets, one foot resting on the second step of the stairs. She had been silent for a long time. Her face had the expression often seen in slightly cross-eyed persons who are thinking deeply, a look that appears to be both very wise and very crazy. At last she said: "I don't know your name."

"I'm Lymon Willis," said the hunchback.

"Well, come on in," she said. "Some supper was left in the stove and you can eat."

marsh a piece of land that is soft and wet – *dainty* small and pretty – *weaver* person who forms threads into material on a loom (Weber) – *weird* ['wɪəd] strange; unnatural; unusual – *radiance* brightness and warmth – *forehead* ['fɒrɪd] part of the face above the eyes and below the hair – *cross-eyed* having one or both eyes turned in towards the nose

Only a few times in her life had Miss Amelia invited anyone to eat with her, unless she were planning to trick them in some way, or make money out of them. So the men on the porch felt there was something wrong. Later, they said among themselves that she must have been drinking back in the swamp the better part of the afternoon. At any rate she left the porch, and Stumpy MacPhail and the twins went on off home. She bolted the front door and looked all around to see that her goods were in order. Then she went to the kitchen, which was at the back of the store. The hunchback followed her, dragging his suitcase, sniffing and wiping his nose on the sleeve of his dirty coat.

"Sit down," said Miss Amelia. "I'll just warm up what's here."

It was a good meal they had together on that night. Miss Amelia was rich and she did not grudge herself food. There was fried chicken (the breast of which the hunchback took on his own plate), mashed rootabeggars, collard greens, and hot, pale golden, sweet potatoes. Miss Amelia ate slowly and with the relish of a farm hand. She sat with both elbows on the table, bent over the plate, her knees spread wide apart and her feet braced on the rungs of the chair. As for the hunchback, he gulped down his supper as though he had not smelled food in months. During the meal one tear crept down his dingy cheek – but it was just a little leftover tear and meant nothing at all. The lamp on the table was well-trimmed, burning blue at the edges of the wick, and casting a cheerful light in the kitchen. When Miss Amelia had eaten her supper she wiped her plate carefully with a slice of light bread, and then poured her own clear, sweet syrup over the bread. The hunchback did likewise – except that he was more finicky and asked for a new plate. Having finished, Miss Amelia tilted back her chair, tightened her fist, and felt the hard, supple muscles of her

to bolt [bəʊlt] to lock by using a bar – *to drag* to pull a heavy thing along – *to grudge* to be unwilling to give or allow – *rootabeggar* (coll.) yellow turnip – *collard greens* a kind of cabbage (Kohlsorte der Südstaaten) – *relish* a great deal of enjoyment – *to brace* to put or set firmly – *rung* a bar between the legs of a chair – *to gulp down* to swallow hastily – *to trim* (here) to remove by cutting; to adjust to the right size – *wick* a piece of twisted thread in a candle – *finicky* fussy about details – *to tilt* to cause to slope by raising one end (kippen) – *supple* elastic and flexible

right arm beneath the clean, blue cloth of her shirtsleeves – an unconscious habit with her, at the close of a meal. Then she took the lamp from the table and jerked her head toward the staircase as an invitation for the hunchback to follow after her.

Above the store there were the three rooms where Miss Amelia had lived during all her life – two bedrooms with a large parlor in between. Few people had even seen these rooms, but it was generally known that they were well-furnished and extremely clean. And now Miss Amelia was taking up with her a dirty little hunchbacked stranger, come from God knows where. Miss Amelia walked slowly, two steps at a time, holding the lamp high. The hunchback hovered so close behind her that the swinging light made on the staircase wall one great, twisted shadow of the two of them. Soon the premises above the store were dark as the rest of the town.

IV The next morning was serene, with a sunrise of warm purple mixed with rose. In the fields around the town the furrows were newly plowed, and very early the tenants were at work setting out the young, deep green tobacco plants. The wild crows flew down close to the fields, making swift blue shadows on the earth. In town the people set out early with their dinner pails, and the windows of the mill were blinding gold in the sun. The air was fresh and the peach trees light as March clouds with their blossoms.

Miss Amelia came down at about dawn, as usual. She washed her head at the pump and very shortly set about her business. Later in the morning she saddled her mule and went to see about her property, planted with cotton, up near the Forks Falls Road. By noon, of course, everybody had heard about the hunchback who had come to the store in the middle of the night. But no one as yet had seen him. The day soon grew hot and the sky was a rich, midday blue. Still no one had laid an eye on this strange guest. A few people remembered

to jerk [dʒɜːk] to make a short, quick movement – *parlor* room for receiving guests, reading, etc. – *to hover* (here) to stay in one position – *premises* ['premɪsiːz] (here) apartment – *serene* [sɪ'riːn] completely calm and peaceful – *furrow* a long narrow track cut by a plough in a field – *crow* [krəʊ] large black bird – *swift* quick, fast – *mule* the animal which is the young of a donkey and a horse

that Miss Amelia's mother had had a half-sister – but there was some difference of opinion as to whether she had died or had run off with a tobacco stringer. As for the hunchback's claim, everyone thought it was a trumped-up business. And the town, knowing Miss Amelia, decided that surely she had put him out of the house after feeding him. But toward evening, when the sky had whitened, and the shift was done, a woman claimed to have seen a crooked face at the window of one of the rooms up over the store. Miss Amelia herself said nothing. She clerked in the store for a while, argued for an hour with a farmer over a plow shaft, mended some chicken wire, locked up near sundown, and went to her rooms. The town was left puzzled and talkative.

The next day Miss Amelia did not open the store, but stayed locked up inside her premises and saw no one. Now this was the day that the rumor started – the rumor so terrible that the town and all the country about were stunned by it. The rumor was started by a weaver called Merlie Ryan. He is a man of not much account–sallow, shambling, and with no teeth in his head. He has the three-day malaria, which means that every third day the fever comes on him. So on two days he is dull and cross, but on the third day he livens up and sometimes has an idea or two, most of which are foolish. It was while Merlie Ryan was in his fever that he turned suddenly and said:

"I know what Miss Amelia done. She murdered that man for something in that suitcase."

He said this in a calm voice, as a statement of fact. And within an hour the news had swept through the town. It was a fierce and sickly tale the town built up that day. In it were all the things which cause the heart to shiver – a hunchback, a midnight burial in the swamp, the dragging of Miss Amelia through the streets of the town on the way to prison, the squabbles over what would happen to her property – all told in hushed voices and repeated with some fresh and

tobacco stringer person that ties tobacco plants into bundles – *to trump up* to invent falsely and dishonestly – *to clerk* [klɑ:k] to work in an office – *shaft* handle – *rumor* common talk, perhaps untrue; a story that reaches one through this – *to be stunned* to be shocked – *sallow* ['sæləʊ] yellow and unhealthy looking – *to shamble* to walk awkwardly, dragging the feet – *sickly* causing a sick feeling – *squabble* a continuing quarrel over s.th. unimportant

weird detail. It rained and women forgot to bring in the washing from the lines. One or two mortals, who were in debt to Miss Amelia, even put on Sunday clothes as though it were a holiday. People clustered together on the main street, talking and watching the store.

It would be untrue to say that all the town took part in this evil festival. There were a few sensible men who reasoned that Miss Amelia, being rich, would not go out of her way to murder a vagabond for a few trifles of junk. In the town there were even three good people, and they did not want this crime, not even for the sake of the interest and the great commotion it would entail; it gave them no pleasure to think of Miss Amelia holding to the bars of the penitentiary and being electrocuted in Atlanta. These good people judged Miss Amelia in a different way from what the others judged her. When a person is as contrary in every single respect as she was and when the sins of a person have amounted to such a point that they can hardly be remembered all at once – then this person plainly requires a special judgment. They remembered that Miss Amelia had been born dark and somewhat queer of face, raised motherless by her father who was a solitary man, that early in youth she had grown to be six feet two inches tall which in itself is not natural for a woman, and that her ways and habits of life were too peculiar ever to reason about. Above all, they remembered her puzzling marriage, which was the most unreasonable scandal ever to happen in this town.

So these good people felt toward her something near to pity. And when she was out on her wild business, such as rushing in a house to drag forth a sewing machine in payment for a debt, or getting herself worked up over some matter concerning the law – they had toward her a feeling which was a mixture of exasperation, a ridiculous little inside tickle, and a deep, unnamable sadness. But enough of the good

mortal (poet.) human being – *to cluster together* to gather – *to entail* to cause; to make s.th. necessary – *to electrocute* to kill by passing electricity through the body – *Atlanta* capital of the state of Georgia – *sewing-machine* ['səʊɪŋməˌʃi:n] a machine for stitching material (Nähmaschine) – *debt* [det] s.th. owed to s.o. else – *exasperation* [ɪgˌzæspə'reɪʃn] state of being annoyed or angry – *ridiculous* deserving unkind laughter; silly – *tickle* feeling of delight or amusement

people, for there were only three of them; the rest of the town was making a holiday of this fancied crime the whole of the afternoon.

Miss Amelia herself, for some strange reason, seemed unaware of all this. She spent most of her day upstairs. When down in the store, she prowled around peacefully, her hands deep in the pockets of her overalls and head bent so low that her chin was tucked inside the collar of her shirt. There was no bloodstain on her anywhere. Often she stopped and just stood somberly looking down at the cracks in the floor, twisting a lock of her shortcropped hair, and whispering something to herself. But most of the day was spent upstairs.

Dark came on. The rain that afternoon had chilled the air, so that the evening was bleak and gloomy as in wintertime. There were no stars in the sky, and a light, icy drizzle had set in. The lamps in the houses made mournful, wavering flickers when watched from the street. A wind had come up, not from the swamp side of the town but from the cold black pinewoods to the north.

The clocks in the town struck eight. Still nothing had happened. The bleak night, after the gruesome talk of the day, put a fear in some people, and they stayed home close to the fire. Others were gathered in groups together. Some eight or ten men had convened on the porch of Miss Amelia's store. They were silent and were indeed just waiting about. They themselves did not know what they were waiting for, but it was this: in times of tension, when some great action is impending, men gather and wait in this way. And after a time there will come a moment when all together they will act in unison, not from thought or from the will of any one man, but as though their instincts had merged together so that the decision belongs to no single one of them, but to the group as a whole. At such a time, no individual hesitates. And whether the matter will be

to prowl around to move about in a quiet way trying not to be seen or heard – *sombre* ['sɒmbə] sadly serious – *short-cropped* cut short – *to chill* to cause to become cold – *mournful* ['mɔ:nfʊl] expressing sorrow or grief – *to waver* (here) to burn unsteadily – *flicker* unsteady movement – *gruesome* terrible to the senses – *to convene* [kən'vi:n] to meet, to come together – *to impend* to be about to happen – *unison* ['ju:nɪzən] perfect agreement, harmony – *to merge* to become part of s.th. else

settled peaceably, or whether the joint action will result in ransacking, violence, and crime, depends on destiny. So the men waited soberly on the porch of Miss Amelia's store, not one of them realizing what they would do, but knowing inwardly that they must wait, and that the time had almost come.

Now the door to the store was open. Inside it was bright and natural-looking. To the left was the counter where slabs of white meat, rock candy, and tobacco were kept. Behind this were shelves of salted white meat and meal. The right side of the store was mostly filled with farm implements and such. At the back of the store, to the left, was the door leading up the stairs, and it was open. And at the far right of the store there was another door which led to a little room that Miss Amelia called her office. This door was also open. And at eight o'clock that evening Miss Amelia could be seen there sitting before her rolltop desk, figuring with a fountain pen and some pieces of paper.

The office was cheerfully lighted, and Miss Amelia did not seem to notice the delegation on the porch. Everything around her was in great order, as usual. This office was a room well-known, in a dreadful way, throughout the country. It was there Miss Amelia transacted all business. On the desk was a carefully covered typewriter which she knew how to run, but used only for the most important documents. In the drawers were literally thousands of papers, all filed according to the alphabet. This office was also the place where Miss Amelia received sick people, for she enjoyed doctoring and did a great deal of it. Two whole shelves were crowded with bottles and various paraphernalia. Against the wall was a bench where the patients sat. She could sew up a wound with a burnt needle so that it would not turn green. For burns she had a cool, sweet syrup. For unlocated sickness there were any number of different medicines which she had brewed herself from unknown recipes. They

to ransack to search through and rob a place – *destiny* power believed to control events – *slab* a thick piece of s.th. – *rock candy* sweets in large, hard crystals – *implement* a tool or instrument – *rolltop desk* a desk whose cover rolls back – *to figure* to calculate – *to file* to store papers away in an orderly manner – *paraphernalia* [ˌpærəfəˈneɪlɪə] a number of small articles needed for some skill or work

wrenched loose the bowels very well, but they could not be given to small children, as they caused bad convulsions; for them she had an entirely separate draught, gentler and sweet-flavored. Yes, all in all, she was considered a good doctor. Her hands, though very large and bony, had a light touch about them. She possessed great imagination and used hundreds of different cures. In the face of the most dangerous and extraordinary treatment she did not hesitate, and no disease was so terrible but what she would undertake to cure it. In this there was one exception. If a patient came with a female complaint she could do nothing. Indeed at the mere mention of the words her face would slowly darken with shame, and she would stand there craning her neck against the collar of her shirt, or rubbing her swamp boots together, for all the world like a great, shamed, dumb-tongued child. But in other matters people trusted her. She charged no fees whatsoever and always had a raft of patients.

On this evening, Miss Amelia wrote with her fountain pen a good deal. But even so she could not be forever unaware of the group waiting out there on the dark porch, and watching her. From time to time she looked up and regarded them steadily. But she did not holler out to them to demand why they were loafing around her property like a sorry bunch of gabbies. Her face was proud and stern, as it always was when she sat at the desk of her office. After a time their peering in like that seemed to annoy her. She wiped her cheek with a red handkerchief, got up, and closed the office door.

Now to the group on the porch this gesture acted as a signal. The time had come. They had stood for a long while with the night raw and gloomy in the street behind them. They had waited long and just at that moment the instinct to act came on them. All at once, as though moved by one will, they walked into the store. At that moment the eight men looked very much alike – all wearing blue

bowels ['baʊəlz] a long pipe continuing down from the stomach and leading the waste matter out of the body (Darm) – *convulsions* [kən'vʌlʃənz] an unnaturally violent and sudden movement – *draught* [drɑ:ft] a mouthful of liquid – *to crane* to stretch out (one's neck) in order to get a better view – *a raft of* a large number of – *to holler* (coll.) to shout out – *to loaf* to waste time by not working when one should – *bunch of gabbies* a group of people inclined to chatter – *stern* showing firmness, esp. with disapproval

overalls, most of them with whitish hair, all pale of face, and all with a set, dreaming look in the eye. What they would have done next no one knows. But at that instant there was a noise at the head of the staircase. The men looked up and then stood dumb with shock. It was the hunchback, whom they had already murdered in their minds. Also, the creature was not at all as had been pictured to them – not a pitiful and dirty little chatterer, alone and beggared in this world. Indeed, he was like nothing any man among them had ever beheld until that time. The room was still as death.

The hunchback came down slowly with the proudness of one who owns every plank of the floor beneath his feet. In the past days he had greatly changed. For one thing he was clean beyond words. He still wore his little coat, but it was brushed off and neatly mended. Beneath this was a fresh red and black checkered shirt belonging to Miss Amelia. He did not wear trousers such as ordinary men are meant to wear, but a pair of tightfitting little knee-length breeches. On his skinny legs he wore black stockings, and his shoes were of a special kind, being queerly shaped, laced up over the ankles, and newly cleaned and polished with wax. Around his neck, so that his large, pale ears were almost completely covered, he wore a shawl of lime-green wool, the fringes of which almost touched the floor.

The hunchback walked down the store with his stiff little strut and then stood in the center of the group that had come inside. They cleared a space about him and stood looking with hands loose at their sides and eyes wide open. The hunchback himself got his bearings in an odd manner. He regarded each person steadily at his own eye-level, which was about belt line for an ordinary man. Then with shrewd deliberation he examined each man's lower regions – from the waist to the sole of the shoe. When he had satisfied himself he

dumb [dʌm] unable to speak – *to beggar* to make very poor – *to checker* to cover with a pattern of differently coloured squares – *breeches* ['brɪtʃɪz] short trousers for men fastened at the knees – *queer* strange – *to lace up* to fasten with a string – *lime* a type of tree which bears a small juicy green fruit with sour taste (Limone) – *strut* a proud way of walking – *loose* [lu:s] free from control – *to get one's bearings* ['beərɪŋz] to get an understanding of one's position or the state of affairs – *shrewd* clever – *deliberation* the act of carefully thinking about a matter

closed his eyes for a moment and shook his head, as though in his opinion what he had seen did not amount to much. Then with assurance, only to confirm himself, he tilted back his head and took in the halo of faces around him with one long, circling stare. There was a half-filled sack of guano on the left side of the store, and when he had found his bearings in this way, the hunchback sat down upon it. Cozily settled, with his little legs crossed, he took from his coat pocket a certain object.

Now it took some moments for the men in the store to regain their ease. Merlie Ryan, he of the three-day fever who had started the rumor that day, was the first to speak. He looked at the object which the hunchback was fondling, and said in a hushed voice:

"What is it you have there?"

Each man knew well what it was the hunchback was handling. For it was the snuffbox which had belonged to Miss Amelia's father. The snuffbox was of blue enamel with a dainty embellishment of wrought gold on the lid. The group knew it well and marveled. They glanced warily at the closed office door, and heard the low sound of Miss Amelia whistling to herself.

"Yes, what is it, Peanut?"

The hunchback looked up quickly and sharpened his mouth to speak. "Why, this is a lay-low to catch meddlers."

The hunchback reached in the box with his scrambly little fingers and ate something, but he offered no one around him a taste. It was not even proper snuff which he was taking, but a mixture of sugar and cocoa. This he took, though, as snuff, pocketing a little wad of it beneath his lower lip and licking down neatly into this with a flick of his tongue which made a frequent grimace come over his face.

"The very teeth in my head have always tasted sour to me," he said in explanation. "That is the reason why I take this kind of sweet snuff."

halo ['heɪləʊ] a golden circle representing light around the heads of holy persons (Heiligenschein) – *guano* the waste droppings of seabirds used to enrich the soil where plants are grown – *cozy* warm and comfortable – *to fondle* to touch in a loving way – *enamel* [ɪ'næməl] glassy substance which is put onto objects such as kitchen pots (Emaille) – *wrought* [rɔ:t] (metal) beaten into shape – *lay-low* (sl.) trap – *meddler* person who is interested in s.o. else's business

The group still clustered around, feeling somewhat gawky and bewildered. This sensation never quite wore off, but it was soon tempered by another feeling – an air of intimacy in the room and a vague festivity. Now the names of the men of the group there on that evening were as follows: Hasty Malone, Robert Calvert Hale, Merlie Ryan, Reverend T. M. Willin, Rosser Cline, Rip Wellborn, Henry Ford Crimp, and Horace Wells. Except for Reverend Willin, they are all alike in many ways as has been said – all having taken pleasure from something or other, all having wept and suffered in some way, most of them tractable unless exasperated. Each of them worked in the mill, and lived with others in a two- or three-room house for which the rent was ten dollars or twelve dollars a month. All had been paid that afternoon, for it was Saturday. So, for the present, think of them as a whole.

The hunchback, however, was already sorting them out in his mind. Once comfortably settled he began to chat with everyone, asking questions such as if a man was married, how old he was, how much his wages came to in an average week, et cetera – picking his way along to inquiries which were downright intimate. Soon the group was joined by others in the town, Henry Macy, idlers who had sensed something extraordinary, women come to fetch their men who lingered on, and even one loose, towhead child who tiptoed into the store, stole a box of animal crackers, and made off very quietly. So the premises of Miss Amelia were soon crowded, and she herself had not yet opened her office door.

There is a type of person who has a quality about him that sets him apart from other and more ordinary human beings. Such a person has an instinct which is usually found only in small children, an instinct to establish immediate and vital contact between himself and all things in the world. Certainly the hunchback was of this type. He had only been in the store half an hour before an immediate contact had been established between him and each other individual. It was as though he had lived in the town for years, was a well-known

scrambly clumsy, grasping – *gawky* awkward in movement – *tractable* that can be easily controlled or governed – *to exasperate* [ɪg'zæspəreɪt] to annoy or make angry – *towhead* of a person having pale yellow hair

character, and had been sitting and talking there on that guano sack for countless evenings. This, together with the fact that it was Saturday night, could account for the air of freedom and illicit gladness in the store. There was a tension, also, partly because of the oddity of the situation and because Miss Amelia was still closed off in her office and had not yet made her appearance.

She came out that evening at ten o'clock. And those who were expecting some drama at her entrance were disappointed. She opened the door and walked in with her slow, gangling swagger. There was a streak of ink on one side of her nose, and she had knotted the red handkerchief about her neck. She seemed to notice nothing unusual. Her gray, crossed eyes glanced over to the place where the hunchback was sitting, and for a moment lingered there. The rest of the crowd in her store she regarded with only a peaceable surprise.

"Does anyone want waiting on?" she asked quietly.

There were a number of customers, because it was Saturday night, and they all wanted liquor. Now Miss Amelia had dug up an aged barrel only three days past and had siphoned it into bottles back by the still. This night she took the money from the customers and counted it beneath the bright light. Such was the ordinary procedure. But after this what happened was not ordinary. Always before, it was necessary to go around to the dark back yard, and there she would hand out your bottle through the kitchen door. There was no feeling of joy in the transaction. After getting his liquor the customer walked off into the night. Or, if his wife would not have it in the home, he was allowed to come back around to the front porch of the store and guzzle there or in the street. Now, both the porch and the street before it were the property of Miss Amelia, and no mistake about it – but she did not regard them as her premises; the premises began at the front door and took in the entire inside of the building. There she had never allowed liquor to be opened or drunk by anyone but herself. Now for the first time she broke this rule. She went to

illicit against a law or rule – *tension* a feeling of nervous anxiety, worry, or pressure – *swagger* walking in a proud, self-important way – *barrel* a round wooden container for liquids, such as wine or oil – *to siphon* ['saɪfən] to draw off through a tube or tap – *to guzzle* (here) to drink eagerly and greedily

the kitchen, with the hunchback close at her heels, and she brought back the bottles into the warm, bright store. More than that she furnished some glasses and opened two boxes of crackers so that they were there hospitably in a platter on the counter and anyone who wished could take one free.

She spoke to no one but the hunchback, and she only asked him in a somewhat harsh and husky voice: "Cousin Lymon, will you have yours straight, or warmed in a pan with water on the stove?"

"If you please, Amelia," the hunchback said. (And since what time had anyone presumed to address Miss Amelia by her bare name, without a title of respect? – Certainly not her bridegroom and her husband of ten days. In fact, not since the death of her father, who for some reason had always called her Little, had anyone dared to address her in such a familiar way.) "If you please, I'll have it warmed."

Now, this was the beginning of the café. It was as simple as that. Recall that the night was gloomy as in wintertime, and to have sat around the property outside would have made a sorry celebration. But inside there was company and a genial warmth. Someone had rattled up the stove in the rear, and those who bought bottles shared their liquor with friends. Several women were there and they had twists of licorice, a Nehi, or even a swallow of the whisky. The hunchback was still a novelty and his presence amused everyone. The bench in the office was brought in, together with several extra chairs. Other people leaned against the counter or made themselves comfortable on barrels and sacks. Nor did the opening of liquor on the premises cause any rambunctiousness, indecent giggles, or misbehavior whatsoever. On the contrary the company was polite even to the point of a certain timidness. For people in this town were then unused to gathering together for the sake of pleasure. They met to

heel back part of the foot – *husky* difficult to hear and breathy, as if the throat were dry – *genial* ['dʒi:nɪəl] cheerful and kind; good-tempered – *to rattle up* (here) to start a fire – *licorice* sweet black substance produced from a type of plant used as medicine or in sweets (Lakritze) – *Nehi* soft drink – *rambunctiousness* [ræm'bʌŋkʃəsnəs] (humorous) noisy and lively behaviour – *giggles* laughter which is repeated in an uncontrolled manner, esp. by young girls

work in the mill. Or on Sunday there would be an all-day camp meeting – and though that is a pleasure, the intention of the whole affair is to sharpen your view of Hell and put into you a keen fear of the Lord Almighty. But the spirit of a café is altogether different. Even the richest, greediest old rascal will behave himself, insulting no one in a proper café. And poor people look about them gratefully and pinch up the salt in a dainty and modest manner. For the atmosphere of a proper café implies these qualities: fellowship, the satisfactions of the belly, and a certain gaiety and grace of behavior. This had never been told to the gathering in Miss Amelia's store that night. But they knew it of themselves, although never, of course, until that time had there been a café in the town.

Now, the cause of all this, Miss Amelia, stood most of the evening in the doorway leading to the kitchen. Outwardly she did not seem changed at all. But there were many who noticed her face. She watched all that went on, but most of the time her eyes were fastened lonesomely on the hunchback. He strutted about the store, eating from his snuffbox, and being at once sour and agreeable. Where Miss Amelia stood, the light from the chinks of the stove cast a glow, so that her brown, long face was somewhat brightened. She seemed to be looking inward. There was in her expression pain, perplexity, and uncertain joy. Her lips were not so firmly set as usual, and she swallowed often. Her skin had paled and her large empty hands were sweating. Her look that night, then, was the lonesome look of the lover.

This opening of the café came to an end at midnight. Everyone said good-bye to everyone else in a friendly fashion. Miss Amelia shut the front door of her premises, but forgot to bolt it. Soon everything – the main street with its three stores, the mill, the houses – all the town, in fact – was dark and silent. And so ended three days and nights in which had come an arrival of a stranger, an unholy holiday, and the start of the café.

camp meeting (AE) a religious meeting lasting several days, held in a large tent and attended by people who camp in the surrounding area – *rascal* bad, dishonest person – *chink* small gap through which light comes

V Now time must pass. For the next four years are much alike. There are great changes, but these changes are brought about bit by bit, in simple steps which in themselves do not appear to be important. The hunchback continued to live with Miss Amelia. The café expanded in a gradual way. Miss Amelia began to sell her liquor by the drink, and some tables were brought into the store. There were customers every evening, and on Saturday a great crowd. Miss Amelia began to serve fried catfish suppers at fifteen cents a plate. The hunchback cajoled her into buying a fine mechanical piano. Within two years the place was a store no longer, but had been converted into a proper café, open every evening from six until twelve o'clock.

Each night the hunchback came down the stairs with the air of one who has a grand opinion of himself. He always smelled slightly of turnip greens, as Miss Amelia rubbed him night and morning with pot liquor to give him strength. She spoiled him to a point beyond reason, but nothing seemed to strengthen him; food only made his hump and his head grow larger while the rest of him remained weakly and deformed. Miss Amelia was the same in appearance. During the week she still wore swamp boots and overalls, but on Sunday she put on a dark red dress that hung on her in a most peculiar fashion. Her manners, however, and her way of life were greatly changed. She still loved a fierce lawsuit, but she was not so quick to cheat her fellow man and to exact cruel payments. Because the hunchback was so extremely sociable, she even went about a little – to revivals, to funerals, and so forth. Her doctoring was as successful as ever, her liquor even finer than before, if that were possible. The café itself proved profitable and was the only place of pleasure for many miles around.

So for the moment regard these years from random and disjointed views. See the hunchback marching in Miss Amelia's footsteps when

catfish type of large-headed fish (Wels) – *to cajole s.o. into doing s.th.* [kə'dʒəʊl] to persuade by praise or deceit – *pot liquor* (dial.) the liquid left after meat and vegetables have been cooked – *to cheat* to take from s.o. unfairly and dishonestly – *to exact* [ɪg'zækt] to demand and obtain by force and threats – *random* made or done without plan – *disjointed* (of words and ideas) not well connected; not following in reasonable order

on a red winter morning they set out for the pinewoods to hunt. See them working on her properties – with Cousin Lymon standing by and doing absolutely nothing, but quick to point out any laziness among the hands. On autumn afternoons they sat on the back steps chopping sugar cane. The glaring summer days they spent back in the swamp where the water cypress is a deep black green, where beneath the tangled swamp trees there is a drowsy gloom. When the path leads through a bog or a stretch of blackened water see Miss Amelia bend down to let Cousin Lymon scramble on her back – and see her wading forward with the hunchback settled on her shoulders, clinging to her ears or to her broad forehead. Occasionally Miss Amelia cranked up the Ford which she had bought and treated Cousin Lymon to a picture-show in Cheehaw, or to some distant fair or cockfight; the hunchback took a passionate delight in spectacles. Of course, they were in their café every morning, they would often sit for hours together by the fireplace in the parlor upstairs. For the hunchback was sickly at night and dreaded to lie looking into the dark. He had a deep fear of death. And Miss Amelia would not leave him by himself to suffer with this fright. It may even be reasoned that the growth of the café came about mainly on this account; it was a thing that brought him company and pleasure and that helped him through the night. So compose from such flashes an image of these years as a whole. And for a moment let it rest.

VI Now some explanation is due for all this behavior. The time has come to speak about love. For Miss Amelia loved Cousin Lymon. So much was clear to everyone. They lived in the same house together and were never seen apart. Therefore, according to Mrs. MacPhail, a warty-nosed old busybody who is continually moving her sticks of furniture from one part of the front room to another; according to her and to certain others, these two were living in sin. If they were related, they were only a cross between first and second cousins, and even that could in no way be proved. Now, of course, Miss Amelia was a powerful blunderbuss of a person, more than six feet tall – and

to chop to cut by repeatedly striking – *to crank up* (here) to start – *warty* having a small hard ugly swelling on the skin (warzig) – *to live in sin* to live together as if married – *blunderbuss* a large, clumsy person

Cousin Lymon a weakly little hunchback reaching only to her waist. But so much the better for Mrs. Stumpy MacPhail and her cronies, for they and their kind glory in conjunctions which are ill-matched and pitiful. So let them be. The good people thought that if those two had found some satisfaction of the flesh between themselves, then it was a matter concerning them and God alone. All sensible people agreed in their opinion about this conjecture – and their answer was a plain, flat *no*. What sort of thing, then, was this love?

First of all, love is a joint experience between two persons – but the fact that it is a joint experience does not mean that it is a similar experience to the two people involved. There are the lover and the beloved, but these two come from different countries. Often the beloved is only a stimulus for all the stored-up love which has lain quiet within the lover for a long time hitherto. And somehow every lover knows this. He feels in his soul that his love is a solitary thing. He comes to know a new, strange loneliness and it is this knowledge which makes him suffer. So there is only one thing for the lover to do. He must house his love within himself as best he can; he must create for himself a whole new inward world – a world intense and strange, complete in himself. Let it be added here that this lover about whom we speak need not necessarily be a young man saving for a wedding ring – this lover can be man, woman, child, or indeed any human creature on this earth.

Now, the beloved can also be of any description. The most outlandish people can be the stimulus for love. A man may be a doddering great-grandfather and still love only a strange girl he saw in the streets of Cheehaw one afternoon two decades past. The preacher may love a fallen woman. The beloved may be treacherous, greasy-headed, and given to evil habits. Yes, and the lover may see this as clearly as anyone else – but that does not affect the evolution of his love one whit. A most mediocre person can be the object of a love

crony (coll.) a friend or companion – *conjecture* the formation of an opinion from uncertain information – *joint* shared by two or more people – *outlandish* strange, looking as if it comes from a foreign country – *doddering* (coll.) weak, shaky, and slow – *treacherous* ['tretʃərəs] unfaithful, not to be trusted or relied upon – *greasy-headed* ['gri:sɪ] having oily hair – *whit* (coll.) (by) a small amount – *mediocre* [ˌmi:dɪ'əʊkə] of not very good quality

which is wild, extravagant, and beautiful as the poison lilies of the swamp. A good man may be the stimulus for a love both violent and debased, or a jabbering madman may bring about in the soul of someone a tender and simple idyll. Therefore, the value and quality of any love is determined solely by the lover himself.

It is for this reason that most of us would rather love than be loved. Almost everyone wants to be the lover. And the curt truth is that, in a deep secret way, the state of being beloved is intolerable to many. The beloved fears and hates the lover, and with the best of reasons. For the lover is forever trying to strip bare his beloved. The lover craves any possible relation with the beloved, even if this experience can cause him only pain.

It has been mentioned before that Miss Amelia was once married. And this curious episode might as well be accounted for at this point. Remember that it all happened long ago, and that it was Miss Amelia's only personal contact, before the hunchback came to her, with this phenomenon – love.

The town then was the same as it is now, except there were two stores instead of three and the peach trees along the street were more crooked and smaller than they are now. Miss Amelia was nineteen years old at the time, and her father had been dead many months. There was in the town at that time a loom-fixer named Marvin Macy. He was the brother of Henry Macy, although to know them you would never guess that those two could be kin. For Marvin Macy was the handsomest man in this region – being six feet one inch tall, hard-muscled, and with slow gray eyes and curly hair. He was well off, made good wages, and had a gold watch which opened in the back to a picture of a waterfall. From the outward and worldly point of view Marvin Macy was a fortunate fellow; he needed to bow and scrape to no one and always got just what he wanted. But from a

to debase [–'–] to lower in personal quality or in the opinion of others – *to jabber* to say s.th. quickly and not clearly – *idyll* ['ɪdɪl] a simple, happy period of life, often in the country – *curt* rudely short in speech; too short to be polite – *to crave* to want s.th. very much – *loom-fixer* man who repairs looms – *handsomest* best-looking – *to bow and scrape* to be excessively polite

more serious and thoughtful viewpoint Marvin Macy was not a person to be envied, for he was an evil character. His reputation was as bad, if not worse, than that of any young man in the county. For years, when he was a boy, he had carried about with him the dried and salted ear of a man he had killed in a razor fight. He had chopped off the tails of squirrels in the pinewoods just to please his fancy, and in his left hip pocket he carried forbidden marijuana weed to tempt those who were discouraged and drawn toward death. Yet in spite of his well-known reputation he was the beloved of many females in this region – and there were at the time several young girls who were clean-haired and soft-eyed, with tender sweet little buttocks and charming ways. These gentle young girls he degraded and shamed. Then finally, at the age of twenty-two, this Marvin Macy chose Miss Amelia. That solitary, gangling, queer-eyed girl was the one he longed for. Nor did he want her because of her money, but solely out of love.

And love changed Marvin Macy. Before the time when he loved Miss Amelia it could be questioned if such a person had within him a heart and soul. Yet there is some explanation for the ugliness of his character, for Marvin Macy had had a hard beginning in this world. He was one of seven unwanted children whose parents could hardly be called parents at all; these parents were wild younguns who liked to fish and roam around the swamp. Their own children, and there was a new one almost every year, were only a nuisance to them. At night when they came home from the mill they would look at the children as though they did not know wherever they had come from. If the children cried they were beaten, and the first thing they learned in this world was to seek the darkest corner of the room and try to hide themselves as best they could. They were as thin as little whitehaired ghosts, and they did not speak, not even to each other. Finally, they were abandoned by their parents altogether and left to the mercies of the town. It was a hard winter, with the mill closed down almost three months, and much misery everywhere. But this

squirrel animal with long furry tail that climbs trees and eats nuts – *weed* wild plant (Unkraut) – *to degrade* [–'–] to bring down in the opinion of others or in self-respect – *nuisance* ['nju:səns] a person that causes trouble – *to leave to s.o.'s mercies* to leave to the cruel control of

is not a town to let white orphans perish in the road before your eyes. So here is what came about: the eldest child, who was eight years old, walked into Cheehaw and disappeared – perhaps he took a freight train somewhere and went out into the world, nobody knows. Three other children were boarded out amongst the town, being sent around from one kitchen to another, and as they were delicate they died before Easter time. The last two children were Marvin Macy and Henry Macy, and they were taken into a home. There was a good woman in the town named Mrs. Mary Hale, and she took Marvin Macy and Henry Macy and loved them as her own. They were raised in her household and treated well.

But the hearts of small children are delicate organs. A cruel beginning in this world can twist them into curious shapes. The heart of a hurt child can shrink so that forever afterward it is hard and pitted as the seed of a peach. Or again, the heart of such a child may fester and swell until it is a misery to carry within the body, easily chafed and hurt by the most ordinary things. This last is what happened to Henry Macy, who is so opposite to his brother, is the kindest and gentlest man in town. He lends his wages to those who are unfortunate, and in the old days he used to care for the children whose parents were at the café on Saturday night. But he is a shy man, and he has the look of one who has a swollen heart and suffers. Marvin Macy, however, grew to be bold and fearless and cruel. His heart turned tough as the horns of Satan, and until the time when he loved Miss Amelia he brought to his brother and the good woman who raised him nothing but shame and trouble.

But love reversed the character of Marvin Macy. For two years he loved Miss Amelia, but he did not declare himself. He would stand near the door of her premises, his cap in his hand, his eyes meek and longing and misty gray. He reformed himself completely. He was good to his brother and foster-mother, and he saved his wages and

to perish to die – *to board* to supply meals and lodging – *delicate* easily falling ill – *to fester* to become infected and diseased – *to swell* to increase in fullness and roundness – *to chafe* to become impatient and annoyed – *to declare o.s.* to state clearly one's intentions (as to marrying a partner) – *meek* gentle in nature – *misty* foggy (neblig) – *foster-mother* woman that gives parental care although the (foster-)child is not of her family (Pflegemutter)

learned thrift. Moreover, he reached out toward God. No longer did he lie around on the floor of the front porch all day Sunday, singing and playing his guitar; he attended church services and was present at all religious meetings. He learned good manners: he trained himself to rise and give his chair to a lady, and he quit swearing and fighting and using holy names in vain. So for two years he passed through this transformation and improved his character in every way. Then at the end of the two years he went one evening to Miss Amelia, carrying a bunch of swamp flowers, a sack of chitterlins, and a silver ring – that night Marvin Macy declared himself.

And Miss Amelia married him. Later everyone wondered why. Some said it was because she wanted to get herself some wedding presents. Others believed it came about through the nagging of Miss Amelia's great-aunt in Cheehaw, who was a terrible old woman. Anyway, she strode with great steps down the aisle of the church wearing her dead mother's bridal gown, which was of yellow satin and at least twelve inches too short for her. It was a winter afternoon and the clear sun shone through the ruby windows of the church and put a curious glow on the pair before the altar. As the marriage lines were read Miss Amelia kept making an odd gesture – she would rub the palm of her right hand down the side of her satin wedding gown. She was reaching for the pocket of her overalls, and being unable to find it her face became impatient, bored, and exasperated. At last when the lines were spoken and the marriage prayer was done Miss Amelia hurried out of the church, not taking the arm of her husband, but walking at least two paces ahead of him.

The church is no distance from the store so the bride and groom walked home. It is said that on the way Miss Amelia began to talk about some deal she had worked up with a farmer over a load of kindling wood. In fact, she treated her groom in exactly the same manner she would have used with some customer who had come into the store to buy a pint from her. But so far all had gone decently

thrift wise use of money and goods – *to quit* (coll.) to stop doing s.th. – *to nag* to worry or annoy continuously – *aisle* [aɪl] a passage leading through the length of a church – *satin* ['sætɪn] a kind of very fine smooth cloth mainly of silk – *ruby* the colour of a deep precious stone (rubinrot) – *pace* a single step in walking – *kindling wood* wood for lighting a fire

enough; the town was gratified, as people had seen what this love had done to Marvin Macy and hoped that it might also reform his bride. At least, they counted on the marriage to tone down Miss Amelia's temper, to put a bit of bride-fat on her, and to change her at last into a calculable woman.

They were wrong. The young boys who watched through the window on that night said that this is what actually happened: The bride and groom ate a grand supper prepared by Jeff, the old Negro who cooked for Miss Amelia. The bride took second servings of everything, but the groom picked with his food. Then the bride went about her ordinary business – reading the newspaper, finishing an inventory of the stock in the store, and so forth. The groom hung about in the doorway with a loose, foolish, blissful face and was not noticed. At eleven o'clock the bride took a lamp and went upstairs. The groom followed close behind her. So far all had gone decently enough, but what followed after was unholy.

Within half an hour Miss Amelia had stomped down the stairs in breeches and a khaki jacket. Her face had darkened so that it looked quite black. She slammed the kitchen door and gave it an ugly kick. Then she controlled herself. She poked up the fire, sat down, and put her feet up on the kitchen stove. She read the Farmer's Almanac, drank coffee, and had a smoke with her father's pipe. Her face was hard, stern, and had now whitened to its natural color. Sometimes she paused to jot down some information from the Almanac on a piece of paper. Toward dawn she went into her office and uncovered her typewriter, which she had recently bought and was only just learning how to run. That was the way in which she spent the whole of her wedding night. At daylight she went out to her yard as though nothing whatsoever had occurred and did some carpentering on a rabbit hutch which she had begun the week before and intended to sell somewhere.

to gratify to give pleasure and satisfaction to – *to tone down* to reduce the force of – *calculable* that can be measured and predicted – *to pick with* to eat in small amounts without appetite – *to stomp* to walk with a heavy step – *carpentering* work of a person who can make and repair wooden objects – *hutch* a small cage with one side made of wire netting (Kaninchenstall)

A groom is in a sorry fix when he is unable to bring his well-beloved bride to bed with him, and the whole town knows it. Marvin Macy came down that day still in his wedding finery, and with a sick face. God knows how he had spent the night. He moped about the yard, watching Miss Amelia, but keeping some distance away from her. Then toward noon an idea came to him and he went off in the direction of Society City. He returned with presents – an opal ring, a pink enamel doreen of the sort which was then in fashion, a silver bracelet with two hearts on it, and a box of candy which had cost two dollars and a half. Miss Amelia looked over these fine gifts and opened the box of candy, for she was hungry. The rest of the presents she judged shrewdly for a moment to sum up their value – then she put them in the counter out for sale. The night was spent in much the same manner as the preceding one – except that Miss Amelia brought her feather mattress to make a pallet by the kitchen stove, and she slept fairly well.

Things went on like this for three days. Miss Amelia went about her business as usual, and took great interest in some rumor that a bridge was to be built some ten miles down the road. Marvin Macy still followed her about around the premises, and it was plain from his face how he suffered. Then on the fourth day he did an extremely simple-minded thing: he went to Cheehaw and came back with a lawyer. Then in Miss Amelia's office he signed over to her the whole of his worldly goods, which was ten acres of timberland which he had bought with the money he had saved. She studied the paper sternly to make sure there was no possibility of a trick and filed it soberly in the drawer of her desk. That afternoon Marvin Macy took a quart bottle of whisky and went with it alone out in the swamp while the sun was still shining. Toward evening he came in drunk, went up to Miss Amelia with wet wide eyes, and put his hand on her shoulder. He was trying to tell her something, but before he could open his mouth she had swung once with her fist and hit his face so

sorry fix a very difficult position – *to mope about* to wander about feeling sad – *opal* ['əʊpl] precious stone which looks like milky water with colours in it – *doreen* piece of jewellery – *pallet* ['pælɪt] hard, narrow, uncomfortable bed – *timberland* land with trees supplying wood for building – *quart* about one litre

hard that he was thrown back against the wall and one of his front teeth was broken.

The rest of this affair can only be mentioned in bare outline. After this first blow Miss Amelia hit him whenever he came within arm's reach of her, and whenever he was drunk. At last she turned him off the premises altogether, and he was forced to suffer publicly. During the day he hung around just outside the boundary line of Miss Amelia's property and sometimes with a drawn crazy look he would fetch his rifle and sit there cleaning it, peering at Miss Amelia steadily. If she was afraid she did not show it, but her face was sterner than ever, and often she spat on the ground. His last foolish effort was to climb in the window of her store one night and to sit there in the dark, for no purpose whatsoever, until she came down the stairs next morning. For this Miss Amelia set off immediately to the courthouse in Cheehaw with some notion that she could get him locked in the penitentiary for trespassing. Marvin Macy left the town that day, and no one saw him go, or knew just where he went. On leaving he put a long curious letter, partly written in pencil and partly with ink, beneath Miss Amelia's door. It was a wild love letter – but in it were also included threats, and he swore that in his life he would get even with her. His marriage had lasted for ten days. And the town felt the special satisfaction that people feel when someone has been thoroughly done in by some scandalous and terrible means.

Miss Amelia was left with everything that Marvin Macy had ever owned – his timberwood, his gilt watch, every one of his possessions. But she seemed to attach little value to them and that spring she cut up his Klansman's robe to cover her tobacco plants. So all that he had ever done was to make her richer and to bring her love. But, strange to say, she never spoke of him but with a terrible and spiteful bitterness. She never once referred to him by name but always mentioned him scornfully as "that loom-fixer I was married to."

to trespass ['trespəs] to go onto privately-owned land without permission – *threat* an expression of an intention to hurt or punish – *gilt* shiny material, esp. gold used as a thin covering – *Klansman* member of the Ku Klux Klan. The KKK was founded in Tennessee in 1865.

And later, when horrifying rumors concerning Marvin Macy reached the town, Miss Amelia was very pleased. For the true character of Marvin Macy finally revealed itself, once he had freed himself of his love. He became a criminal whose picture and whose name were in all the papers in the state. He robbed three filling stations and held up the A & P store of Society City with a sawed-off gun. He was suspected of the murder of Slit-Eye Sam who was a noted highjacker. All these crimes were connected with the name of Marvin Macy, so that his evil became famous through many countries. Then finally the law captured him, drunk, on the floor of a tourist cabin, his guitar by his side, and fifty-seven dollars in his right shoe. He was tried, sentenced, and sent off to the penitentiary near Atlanta. Miss Amelia was deeply gratified.

Well, all this happened a long time ago, and it is the story of Miss Amelia's marriage. The town laughed a long time over this grotesque affair. But though the outward facts of this love are indeed sad and ridiculous, it must be remembered that the real story was that which took place in the soul of the lover himself. So who but God can be the final judge of this or any other love? On the very first night of the café there were several who suddenly thought of this broken bridegroom, locked in the gloomy penitentiary, many miles away. And in the years that followed, Marvin Macy was not altogether forgotten in the town. His name was never mentioned in the presence of Miss Amelia or the hunchback. But the memory of his passion and his crimes, and the thought of him trapped in his cell in the penitentiary, was like a troubling undertone beneath the happy love of Miss Amelia and the gaiety of the café. So do not forget this Marvin Macy, as he is to act a terrible part in the story which is yet to come.

VIII During the four years in which the store became a café the rooms upstairs were not changed. This part of the premises remained exactly as it had been all of Miss Amelia's life, as it was in the time of her father, and most likely his father before him. The three rooms, it

highjacker person who takes control of s.th. by force of arms for the purpose of stealing – *bridegroom* (here) a man just married – *to trap* to catch by a trick – *undertone* a hidden meaning

is already known, were immaculately clean. The smallest object had its exact place, and everything was wiped and dusted by Jeff, the servant of Miss Amelia, each morning. The front room belonged to Cousin Lymon – it was the room where Marvin Macy had stayed during the few nights he was allowed on the premises, and before that it was the bedroom of Miss Amelia's father. The room was furnished with a large chifforobe, a bureau covered with a stiff white linen cloth crocheted at the edges, and a marble-topped table. The bed was immense, an old fourposter made of carved, dark rosewood. On it were two feather mattresses, bolsters, and a number of hand-made comforts. The bed was so high that beneath it were two wooden steps – no occupant had ever used these steps before, but Cousin Lymon drew them out each night and walked up in state. Beside the steps, but pushed modestly out of view, there was a china chamber-pot painted with pink roses. No rug covered the dark, polished floor and the curtains were of some white stuff, also crocheted at the edges.

On the other side of the parlor was Miss Amelia's bedroom, and it was smaller and very simple. The bed was narrow and made of pine. There was a bureau for her breeches, shirts, and Sunday dress, and she had hammered two nails in the closet wall on which to hang her swamp boots. There were no curtains, rugs, or ornaments of any kind.

The large middle room, the parlor, was elaborate. The rosewood sofa, upholstered in threadbare green silk, was before the fireplace. Marble-topped tables, two Singer sewing machines, a big vase of pampas grass – everything was rich and grand. The most important

immaculate [ɪ'mækjʊlɪt] clean and unspoilt, pure – *chifforobe* narrow, high chest of drawers with a mirror – *bureau* (AE) a chest of drawers for bedroom use – *to crochet* ['krəʊʃeɪ] to do fancy needle work (häkeln) – *marble* a hard sort of limestone used for building (Marmor) – *fourposter* a bedstead with tall corner posts – *bolster* ['bəʊlstə] a long hard pillow (Keilkissen) – *comfort* a quilted bed covering (Steppdecke) – *in state* ceremoniously – *chamber-pot* round vessel used in the bedroom by children, old, and sick people – *elaborate* [ɪ'læbərət] worked out with care and in great detail – *to upholster* [ʌp'həʊlstə] to fit with soft coverings over filling materials – *pampas grass* tall ornamental grass with sharp-edged blades and silver-white flowers

piece of furniture in the parlor was a big, glass-doored cabinet in which was kept a number of treasures and curios. Miss Amelia had added two objects to this collection – one was a large acorn from a water oak, the other a little velvet box holding two small, grayish stones. Sometimes when she had nothing much to do, Miss Amelia would take out this velvet box and stand by the window with the stones in the palm of her hand, looking down at them with a mixture of fascination, dubious respect, and fear. They were the kidney stones of Miss Amelia herself, and had been taken from her by the doctor in Cheehaw some years ago. It had been a terrible experience, from the first minute to the last, and all she had got out of it were those two little stones; she was bound to set great store by them, or else admit to a mighty sorry bargain. So she kept them and in the second year of Cousin Lymon's stay with her she had them set as ornaments in a watch chain which she gave to him. The other object she had added to the collection, the large acorn, was precious to her – but when she looked at it her face was always saddened and perplexed.

"Amelia, what does it signify?" Cousin Lymon asked her.

"Why, it's just an acorn," she answered. "Just an acorn I picked up on the afternoon Big Papa died."

"How do you mean?" Cousin Lymon insisted.

"I mean it's just an acorn I spied on the ground that day. I picked it up and put it in my pocket. But I don't know why."

"What a peculiar reason to keep it," Cousin Lymon said.

The talks of Miss Amelia and Cousin Lymon in the rooms upstairs, usually in the first few hours of the morning when the hunchback could not sleep, were many. As a rule, Miss Amelia was a silent woman, not letting her tongue run wild on any subject that happened to pop into her head. There were certain topics of conversation, however, in which she took pleasure. All these subjects had

curio an object that is valuable because of its age, rarity, or beauty – *acorn* ['eɪkɔ:n] the fruit or nut of the oak tree – *velvet* fine cloth (Samt) – *dubious* of uncertain value or meaning – *kidney* organ in the lower back area (Niere) – *to set great store by* to feel s.th. to be of great importance – *sorry bargain* a bad buy – *to pop into* to enter unexpectedly

one point in common – they were interminable. She liked to contemplate problems which could be worked over for decades and still remain insoluble. Cousin Lymon, on the other hand, enjoyed talking on any subject whatsoever, as he was a great chatterer. Their approach to any conversation was altogether different. Miss Amelia always kept to the broad, rambling generalities of the matter, going on endlessly in a low, thoughtful voice and getting nowhere – while Cousin Lymon would interrupt her suddenly to pick up, magpie fashion, some detail which, even if unimportant, was at least concrete and bearing on some practical facet close at hand. Some of the favorite subjects of Miss Amelia were: the stars, the reason why Negroes are black, the best treatment for cancer, and so forth. Her father was also an interminable subject which was dear to her.

"Why, Law," she would say to Lymon. "Those days I slept. I'd go to bed just as the lamp was turned on and sleep – why, I'd sleep like I was drowned in warm axle grease. Then come daybreak Big Papa would walk in and put his hand down on my shoulder. 'Get stirring, Little,' he would say. Then later he would holler up the stairs from the kitchen when the stove was hot. 'Fried grits,' he would holler. 'White meat and gravy. Ham and eggs.' And I'd run down the stairs and dress by the hot stove while he was out washing at the pump. Then off we'd go to the still or maybe –"

"The grits we had this morning was poor," Cousin Lymon said. "Fried too quick so that the inside never heated."

"And when Big Papa would run off the liquor in those days –" The conversation would go on endlessly, with Miss Amelia's long legs stretched out before the hearth; for winter or summer there was always a fire in the grate, as Lymon was cold-natured. He sat in a low chair across from her, his feet not quite touching the floor and his torso usually well-wrapped in a blanket or the green wool shawl. Miss Amelia never mentioned her father to anyone else except Cousin Lymon.

interminable (seeming) endless – *to contemplate* to think deeply about – *rambling* disordered and wandering – *magpie* (Elster) (here) a person who likes collecting objects – *to bear on* to show some connection with – *facet* ['fæsɪt] any of the many parts of a subject to be considered; aspect – *to holler* to yell, to shout loudly – *grits* coarsely ground oatmeal – *hearth* [hɑ:θ] fireplace

That was one of the ways in which she showed her love for him. He had her confidence in the most delicate and vital matters. He alone knew where she kept the chart that showed where certain barrels of whisky were buried on a piece of property near by. He alone had access to her bank-book and the key to the cabinet of curios. He took money from the cash register, whole handfuls of it, and appreciated the loud jingle it made inside his pockets. He owned almost everything on the premises, for when he was cross Miss Amelia would prowl about and find him some present – so that now there was hardly anything left close at hand to give him. The only part of her life that she did not want Cousin Lymon to share with her was the memory of her ten-day marriage. Marvin Macy was the one subject that was never, at any time, discussed between the two of them.

IX So let the slow years pass and come to a Saturday evening six years after the time when Cousin Lymon came first to the town. It was August and the sky had burned above the town like a sheet of flame all day. Now the green twilight was near and there was a feeling of repose. The street was coated an inch deep with dry golden dust and the little children ran about half-naked, sneezed often, sweated, and were fretful. The mill had closed down at noon. People in the houses along the main street sat resting on their steps and the women had palmetto fans. At Miss Amelia's there was a sign at the front of the premises saying CAFE. The back porch was cool with latticed shadows and there cousin Lymon sat turning the ice-cream freezer – often he unpacked the salt and ice and removed the dasher to lick a bit and see how the work was coming on. Jeff cooked in the kitchen. Early that morning Miss Amelia had put a notice on the wall of the front porch reading: Chicken Dinner – Twenty Cents Tonite. The

chart map – *jingle* repeated sound produced by coins striking against each other – *to prowl about* to move about in a quiet way trying not to be seen or heard – *to sneeze* to have an uncontrolled burst of air out of the nose – *fretful* complaining because of dissatisfaction – *palmetto* [pæl'metəʊ] (here) leaf of a small palm tree – *lattice* a framework of flat wooden poles crossed over each other with open spaces between (Lattenwerk) – *dasher* a rotating device (Spritzbrett) – *tonite* (AE) tonight

café was already open and Miss Amelia had just finished a period of work in her office. All the eight tables were occupied and from the mechanical piano came a jingling tune.

In a corner near the door and sitting at a table with a child, was Henry Macy. He was drinking a glass of liquor, which was unusual for him, as liquor went easily to his head and made him cry or sing. His face was very pale and his left eye worked constantly in a nervous tic, as it was apt to do when he was agitated. He had come into the café sidewise and silent, and when he was greeted he did not speak. The child next to him belonged to Harace Wells, and he had been left at Miss Amelia's that morning to be doctored.

Miss Amelia came out from her office in good spirits. She attended to a few details in the kitchen and entered the café with the pope's nose of a hen between her fingers, as that was her favorite piece. She looked about the room, saw that in general all was well, and went over to the corner table by Henry Macy. She turned the chair around and sat straddling the back, as she only wanted to pass the time of day and was not yet ready for her supper. There was a bottle of Kroup Kure in the hip pocket of her overalls – a medicine made from whisky, rock candy, and a secret ingredient. Miss Amelia uncorked the bottle and put it to the mouth of the child. Then she turned to Henry Macy and, seeing the nervous winking of his left eye, she asked:

"What ails you?"

Henry Macy seemed on the point of saying something difficult, but, after a long look into the eyes of Miss Amelia, he swallowed and did not speak.

So Miss Amelia returned to her patient. Only the child's head showed above the table top. His face was very red, with the eyelids half-closed and the mouth partly open. He had a large, hard, swollen boil on his thigh, and had been brought to Miss Amelia so that it could be opened. But Miss Amelia used a special method with chil-

agitated troubled; strongly moved – *pope's nose* the rump of a bird (Steiß, Hinterteil) – *to straddle* to sit with one's legs out at the sides (rittlings sitzen) – *Kroup Kure* trade name; croup: an infection of the breathing tract (Krupp); cure: medical treatment – *ingredient* [–'– – –] any of the things that a mixture is made of – *to ail* to trouble – *boil* painful infected swelling

dren; she did not like to see them hurt, struggling, and terrified. So she had kept the child around the premises all day, giving him licorice and frequent doses of the Kroup Kure, and toward evening she tied a napkin around his neck and let him eat his fill of the dinner. Now as he sat at the table his head wobbled slowly from side to side and sometimes as he breathed there came from him a little worn-out grunt.

There was a stir in the café and Miss Amelia looked around quickly. Cousin Lymon had come in. The hunchback strutted into the café as he did every night, and when he reached the exact center of the room he stopped short and looked shrewdly around him, summing up the people and making a quick pattern of the emotional material at hand that night. The hunchback was a great mischief-maker. He enjoyed any kind of to-do, and without saying a word he could set the people at each other in a way that was miraculous. It was due to him that the Rainey twins had quarreled over a jacknife two years past, and had not spoken one word to each other since. He was present at the big fight between Rip Wellborn and Robert Calvert Hale, and every other fight for that matter since he had come into the town. He nosed around everywhere, knew the intimate business of everybody, and trespassed every waking hour. Yet, queerly enough, in spite of this it was the hunchback who was most responsible for the great popularity of the café. Things were never so gay as when he was around. When he walked into the room there was always a quick feeling of tension, because with this busybody about there was never any telling what might descend on you, or what might suddenly be brought to happen in the room. People are never so free with themselves and so recklessly glad as when there is some possibility of commotion or calamity ahead. So when the hunchback marched into the café everyone looked around at him and there was a quick outburst of talking and a drawing of corks.

Lymon waved his hand to Stumpy MacPhail who was sitting with Merlie Ryan and Henry Ford Crimp. "I walked to Rotten Lake today

one's fill as much as one can eat – *to wobble* to move unsteadily – *grunt* short sound like that of a pig – *shrewd* clever in judgment – *pattern* s.th. serving as a model – *mischief-maker* troublemaker – *jackknife* large pocket knife with a folding blade – *recklessly* completely uncaring about danger – *commotion* noisy excitement – *calamity* a terrible event

to fish," he said. "And on the way I stepped over what appeared at first to be a big fallen tree. But then as I stepped over I felt something stir and I taken this second look and there I was straddling this here alligator long as from the front door to the kitchen and thicker than a hog."

The hunchback chattered on. Everyone looked at him from time to time, and some kept track of his chattering and others did not. There were times when every word he said was nothing but lying and bragging. Nothing he said tonight was true. He had lain in bed with a summer quinsy all day long, and had only got up in the late afternoon in order to turn the ice-cream freezer. Everybody knew this, yet he stood there in the middle of the café and held forth with such lies and boasting that it was enough to shrivel the ears.

Miss Amelia watched him with her hands in her pockets and her head turned to one side. There was a softness about her gray, queer eyes and she was smiling gently to herself. Occasionally she glanced from the hunchback to the other people in the café – and then her look was proud, and there was in it the hint of a threat, as though daring anyone to try to hold him to account for all his foolery. Jeff was bringing in the suppers, already served on the plates, and the new electric fans in the café made a pleasant stir of coolness in the air.

"The little youngun is asleep," said Henry Macy finally.

Miss Amelia looked down at the patient beside her, and composed her face for the matter in hand. The child's chin was resting on the table edge and a trickle of spit or Kroup Kure had bubbled from the corner of his mouth. His eyes were quite closed, and a little family of gnats had clustered peacefully in the corners. Miss Amelia put her hand on his head and shook it roughly, but the patient did not awake. So Miss Amelia lifted the child from the table, being careful not to touch the sore part of his leg, and went into the office. Henry Macy followed after her and they closed the office door.

Cousin Lymon was bored that evening. There was not much going on, and in spite of the heat the customers in the café were

hog pig – *to brag* to praise o.s. falsely – *quinsy* ['kwɪnzi:] severe infection of the tonsils (Mandelentzündung) – *to boast* to talk proudly – *to shrivel* to dry out and become smaller – *to compose* to make calm – *gnat* [næt] small insect that stings (Stechmücke) – *to cluster* to gather

good-humored. Henry Ford Crimp and Horace Wells sat at the middle table with their arms around each other, sniggering over some long joke – but when he approached them he could make nothing of it as he had missed the beginning of the story. The moonlight brightened the dusty road, and the dwarfed peach trees were black and motionless: there was no breeze. The drowsy buzz of swamp mosquitoes was like an echo of the silent night. The town seemed dark, except far down the road to the right there was the flicker of a lamp. Somewhere in the darkness a woman sang in a high wild voice and the tune had no start and no finish and was made up of only three notes which went on and on and on. The hunchback stood leaning against the banister of the porch, looking down the empty road as though hoping that someone would come along.

There were footsteps behind him, then a voice: "Cousin Lymon, your dinner is set out upon the table."

"My appetite is poor tonight," said the hunchback, who had been eating sweet snuff all the day. "There is a sourness in my mouth."

"Just a pick," said Miss Amelia. "The breast, the liver, and the heart."

Together they went back into the bright café, and sat down with Henry Macy. Their table was the largest one in the café, and on it there was a bouquet of swamp lilies in a Coca Cola bottle. Miss Amelia had finished with her patient and was satisfied with herself. From behind the closed office door there had come only a few sleepy whimpers, and before the patient could wake up and become terrified it was all over. The child was now slung across the shoulder of his father, sleeping deeply, his little arms dangling loose along his father's back, and his puffed-up face very red – they were leaving the café to go home.

Henry Macy was still silent. He ate carefully, making no noise when he swallowed, and was not a third as greedy as Cousin Lymon who had claimed to have no appetite and was now putting down helping after helping of the dinner. Occasionally Henry Macy looked across at Miss Amelia and again held his peace.

to snigger to laugh secretly – *banister* handrail and posts of a porch or staircase – *puffed-up* swollen

It was a typical Saturday night. An old couple who had come in from the country hesitated for a moment at the doorway, holding each other's hand, and finally decided to come inside. They had lived together so long, this old country couple, that they looked as similar as twins. They were brown, shriveled, and like two little walking peanuts. They left early, and by midnight most of the other customers were gone. Rosser Cline and Merlie Ryan still played checkers, and Stumpy MacPhail sat with a liquor bottle on his table (his wife would not allow it in the home) and carried on peaceable conversations with himself. Henry Macy had not yet gone away, and this was unusual, as he almost always went to bed soon after nightfall. Miss Amelia yawned sleepily, but Lymon was restless and she did not suggest that they close up for the night.

Finally, at one o'clock, Henry Macy looked up at the corner of the ceiling and said quietly to Miss Amelia: "I got a letter today."

Miss Amelia was not one to be impressed by this, because all sorts of business letters and catalogues came addressed to her.

"I got a letter from my brother," said Henry Macy.

The hunchback, who had been goose-stepping about the café with his hands clasped behind his head, stopped suddenly. He was quick to sense any change in the atmosphere of a gathering. He glanced at each face in the room and waited.

Miss Amelia scowled and hardened her right fist. "You are welcome to it," she said.

"He is on parole. He is out of the penitentiary."

The face of Miss Amelia was very dark, and she shivered although the night was warm. Stumpy MacPhail and Merlie Ryan pushed aside their checker game. The café was very quiet.

"Who?" asked Cousin Lymon. His large, pale ears seemed to grow on his head and stiffen. "What?"

Miss Amelia slapped her hands palm down on the table. "Because Marvin Macy is a –" But her voice hoarsened and after a few

shriveled old and wrinkled – *checkers* game played on a board (Damespiel) – *to goose-step* to walk with the legs raised high and kept stiff – *to scowl* to make an angry face – *on parole* letting a person out from prison depending on good behaviour

moments she only said: "He belongs to be in that penitentiary the balance of his life."

"What did he do?" asked Cousin Lymon.

There was a long pause, as no one knew exactly how to answer this. "He robbed three filling stations," said Stumpy MacPhail. But his words did not sound complete and there was a feeling of sins left unmentioned.

The hunchback was impatient. He could not bear to be left out of anything, even a great misery. The name Marvin Macy was unknown to him, but it tantalized him as did any mention of subjects which others knew about and of which he was ignorant – such as any reference to the old sawmill that had been torn down before he came, or a chance word about poor Morris Finestein, or the recollection of any event that had occurred before his time. Aside from this inborn curiosity, the hunchback took a great interest in robbers and crimes of all varieties. As he strutted around the table he was muttering the words "released on parole" and "penitentiary" to himself. But although he questioned insistently, he was unable to find anything, as nobody would dare to talk about Marvin Macy before Miss Amelia in the café.

"The letter did not say very much," said Henry Macy. "He did not say where he was going."

"Humph!" said Amelia, and her face was still hardened and very dark. "He will never set his split hoof on my premises."

She pushed back her chair from the table, and made ready to close the café. Thinking about Marvin Macy may have set her to brooding, for she hauled the cash register back to the kitchen and put it in a private place. Henry Macy went off down the dark road. But Henry Ford Crimp and Merlie Ryan lingered for a time on the front porch. Later Merlie Ryan was to make certain claims, to swear that on that night he had a vision of what was to come. But the town paid no attention, for that was just the sort of thing that Merlie Ryan would claim. Miss Amelia and Cousin Lymon talked for a time in the

for the balance for the rest (of his life) – *to tantalize* to cause to suffer in mind – *insistent* repeatedly making demands – *split hoof* (here) devil's foot – *to brood* to continue to think angrily about s.th. bad – *to haul* to move by pulling

parlor. And when at last the hunchback thought that he could sleep she arranged the mosquito netting over his bed and waited until he had finished with his prayers. Then she put on her long nightgown, smoked two pipes, and only after a long time went to sleep.

X That autumn was a happy time. The crops around the countryside were good, and over at the Forks Falls market the price of tobacco held firm that year. After the long hot summer the first cool days had a clean bright sweetness. Goldenrod grew along the dusty roads, and the sugar cane was ripe and purple. The bus came each day from Cheehaw to carry off a few of the younger children to the consolidated school to get an education. Boys hunted foxes in the pinewoods, winter quilts were aired out on the wash lines, and sweet potatoes bedded in the ground with straw against the colder months to come. In the evening, delicate shreds of smoke rose from the chimneys, and the moon was round and orange in the autumn sky. There is no stillness like the quiet of the first cold nights in the fall. Sometimes, late in the night when there was no wind, there could be heard in the town the thin wild whistle of the train that goes through Society City on its way far off to the North.

For Miss Amelia Evans this was a time of great activity. She was at work from dawn until sundown. She made a new and bigger condenser for her still, and in one week ran off enough liquor to souse the whole country. Her old mule was dizzy from grinding so much sorghum, and she scalded her Mason jars and put away pear preserves. She was looking forward greatly to the first frost, because she had traded for three tremendous hogs, and intended to make much barbecue, chitterlins, and sausage.

goldenrod plant with long branching stalks and small yellow flower heads (Goldrute) – *sugar cane* tall upright tropical plant from whose stems cane sugar is obtained – *consolidated school* public school attended by pupils from several adjoining districts (Mittelpunktschule) – *quilt* bedcover made of two pieces of cloth with soft filling in between (Steppdecke) – *to souse* [saʊs] (sl.) to make drunk – *to grind* to crush into very small pieces (mahlen) – *to scald* [skɔ:ld] to clean with boiling water – *Mason jar* a glass jar (patented in 1858 by John L. Mason) with a screw top used for preserving food

During these weeks there was a quality about Miss Amelia that many people noticed. She laughed often, with a deep ringing laugh, and her whistling had a sassy, tuneful trickery. She was forever trying out her strength, lifting up heavy objects, or poking her tough biceps with her finger. One day she sat down to her typewriter and wrote a story – a story in which there were foreigners, trap doors, and millions of dollars. Cousin Lymon was with her always, traipsing along behind her coat-tails, and when she watched him her face had a bright, soft look, and when she spoke his name there lingered in her voice the undertone of love.

The first cold spell came at last. When Miss Amelia awoke one morning there were frost flowers on the windowpanes, and rime had silvered the patches of grass in the yard. Miss Amelia built a roaring fire in the kitchen stove, then went out of doors to judge the day. The air was cold and sharp, the sky pale green and cloudless. Very shortly people began to come in from the country to find out what Miss Amelia thought of the weather; she decided to kill the biggest hog, and word got round the countryside. The hog was slaughtered and a low oak fire started in the barbecue pit. There was the warm smell of pig blood and smoke in the back yard, the stamp of footsteps, the ring of voices in the winter air. Miss Amelia walked around giving orders and soon most of the work was done.

She had some particular business to do in Cheehaw that day, so after making sure that all was going well, she cranked up her car and got ready to leave. She asked Cousin Lymon to come with her, in fact, she asked him seven times, but he was loath to leave the commotion and wanted to remain. This seemed to trouble Miss Amelia, as she always liked to have him near to her, and was prone to be terribly homesick when she had to go any distance away. But after asking him seven times, she did not urge him any further. Before leaving she found a stick and drew a heavy line all around the barbecue pit, about two feet back from the edge, and told him not to trespass beyond that boundary. She left after dinner and intended to be back before dark.

trap door a small door covering an opening in the roof or floor – *to traipse* [treɪps] (coll.) to walk tiredly – *rime* (poet.) white frost (Rauhreif) – *loath* [ləʊθ] unwilling – *to be prone to* to be inclined to

Now, it is not so rare to have a truck or an automobile pass along the road and through the town on the way from Cheehaw to somewhere else. Every year the tax collector comes to argue with rich people such as Miss Amelia. And if somebody in the town, such as Merlie Ryan, takes a notion that he can connive to get a car on credit, or to pay down three dollars and have a fine electric icebox such as they advertise in the store windows of Cheehaw, then a city man will come out asking meddlesome questions, finding out all his troubles, and ruining his chances of buying anything on the installment plan. Sometimes, especially since they are working on the Forks Falls highway, the cars hauling the chain gang come through the town. And frequently people in automobiles get lost and stop to inquire how they can find the right road again. So, late that afternoon it was nothing unusual to have a truck pass the mill and stop in the middle of the road near the café of Miss Amelia. A man jumped down from the back of the truck, and the truck went on its way.

The man stood in the middle of the road and looked about him. He was a tall man, with brown curly hair, and slow-moving, deep-blue eyes. His lips were red and he smiled the lazy, half-mouthed smile of the braggart. The man wore a red shirt, and a wide belt of tooled leather; he carried a tin suitcase and a guitar. The first person in the town to see this newcomer was Cousin Lymon, who had heard the shifting gears and come around to investigate. The hunchback stuck his head around the corner of the porch, but did not step out altogether into full view. He and the man stared at each other, and it was not the look of two strangers meeting for the first time and swiftly summing up each other. It was a peculiar stare they exchanged between them, like the look of two criminals who recognize each other. Then the man in the red shirt shrugged his left shoulder and turned away. The face of the hunchback was very pale

to take a notion to be of an opinion – *to connive* [kəˈnaɪv] to work secretly for a certain (criminal) purpose – *to pay down* to pay part of the full price with the rest to be paid bit by bit later – *meddlesome* in the habit of being interested in other people's business – *installment* a single payment of several ones which will complete payment (Rate) – *curly* having hair that is twisted into ringlets or coils – *braggart* noisy fellow with a high opinion of himself – *to investigate* to examine the reasons for s.th.

as he watched the man go down the road, and after a few moments he began to follow along carefully, keeping many paces away.

It was immediately known throughout the town that Marvin Macy had come back again. First, he went to the mill, propped his elbows lazily on a window sill and looked inside. He liked to watch others hard at work, as do all born loafers. The mill was thrown into a sort of numb confusion. The dyers left the hot vats, the spinners and weavers forgot about their machines, and even Stumpy MacPhail, who was foreman, did not know exactly what to do. Marvin Macy still smiled his wet half-mouthed smiles, and when he saw his brother, his bragging expression did not change. After looking over the mill Marvin Macy went down the road to the house where he had been raised, and left his suitcase and guitar on the front porch. Then he walked around the millpond, looked over the church, the three stores, and the rest of the town. The hunchback trudged along quietly at some distance behind him, his hands in his pockets, and his little face still very pale.

It had grown late. The red winter sun was setting, and to the west the sky was deep gold and crimson. Ragged chimney swifts flew to their nests; lamps were lighted. Now and then there was the smell of smoke, and the warm rich odor of the barbecue slowly cooking in the pit behind the café. After making the rounds of the town Marvin Macy stopped before Miss Amelia's premises and read the sign above the porch. Then, not hesitating to trespass, he walked through the side yard. The mill whistle blew a thin, lonesome blast, and the day's shift was done. Soon there were others in Miss Amelia's back yard beside Marvin Macy – Henry Ford Crimp, Merlie Ryan, Stumpy MacPhail, and any number of children and people who stood around the edges of the property and looked on. Very little was said. Marvin Macy stood by himself on one side of the pit, and the rest of the people clustered together on the other side. Cousin Lymon stood somewhat apart from everyone, and he did not take his eyes from the face of Marvin Macy.

loafer vagabond – *numb* not able to feel or act – *millpond* part of a stream dammed to drive a water mill (Mühlteich) – *crimson* ['krɪmzən] a deep slightly purplish red colour – *ragged* (of feathers) torn by the wind – *chimney swift* North American bird resembling the swallow – *pit* hole in the ground – *blast* loud sound made by a whistle

"Did you have a good time in the penitentiary?" asked Merlie Ryan, with a silly giggle.

Marvin Macy did not answer. He took from his hip pocket a large knife, opened it slowly, and honed the blade on the seat of his pants. Merlie Ryan grew suddenly very quiet and went to stand directly behind the broad back of Stumpy MacPhail.

XI Miss Amelia did not come home until almost dark. They heard the rattle of her automobile while she was still a long distance away, then the slam of the door and a bumping noise as though she were hauling something up the front steps of her premises. The sun had already set, and in the air there was the blue smoky glow of early winter evenings. Miss Amelia came down the back steps slowly, and the group in her yard waited very quietly. Few people in this world could stand up to Miss Amelia, and against Marvin Macy she had this special and bitter hate. Everyone waited to see her burst into a terrible holler, snatch up some dangerous object, and chase him altogether out of town. At first she did not see Marvin Macy, and her face had the relieved and dreamy expression that was natural to her when she reached home after having gone some distance away.

Miss Amelia must have seen Marvin Macy and Cousin Lymon at the same instant. She looked from one to the other, but it was not the wastrel from the penitentiary on whom she finally fixed her gaze of sick amazement. She, and everyone else, was looking at Cousin Lymon, and he was a sight to see.

The hunchback stood at the end of the pit, his pale face lighted by the soft glow from the smoldering oak fire. Cousin Lymon had a very peculiar accomplishment, which he used whenever he wished to ingratiate himself with someone. He would stand very still, and with just a little concentration, he could wiggle his large pale ears with marvelous quickness and ease. This trick he always used when he wanted to get something special out of Miss Amelia, and to her it

to hone to sharpen – *slam* loud noise of a door closing violently – *to bump* to move with a blow or knock – *wastrel* – worthless person; good-for-nothing – *to smolder* to burn slowly without a flame – *accomplishment* (here) skill – *to ingratiate o.s. with* to make o.s. pleasant to s.o. in order to gain favour – *to wiggle* (coll.) to move

was irresistible. Now as he stood there the hunchback's ears were wiggling furiously on his head, but it was not Miss Amelia at whom he was looking this time. The hunchback was smiling at Marvin Macy with an entreaty that was near to desperation. At first Marvin Macy paid no attention to him, and when he did finally glance at the hunchback it was without any appreciation whatsoever.

"What ails this Brokeback?" he asked with a rough jerk of his thumb.

No one answered. And Cousin Lymon, seeing that his accomplishment was getting him nowhere, added new efforts of persuasion. He fluttered his eyelids, so that they were like pale, trapped moths in his sockets. He scraped his feet around on the ground, waved his hands about, and finally began doing a little trotlike dance. In the last gloomy light of the winter afternoon he resembled the child of a swamphaunt.

Marvin Macy, alone of all the people in the yard, was unimpressed.

"Is the runt throwing a fit?" he asked, and when no one answered he stepped forward and gave Cousin Lymon a cuff on the side of his head. The hunchback staggered, then fell back on the ground. He sat where he had fallen, still looking up at Marvin Macy, and with great effort his ears managed one last forlorn little flap.

Now everyone turned to Miss Amelia to see what she would do. In all these years no one had so much as touched a hair of Cousin Lymon's head, although many had had the itch to do so. If anyone even spoke crossly to the hunchback, Miss Amelia would cut off this rash mortal's credit and find ways of making things go hard for him a long time afterward. So now if Miss Amelia had split open Marvin Macy's head with the ax on the back porch no one would have been surprised. But she did nothing of the kind.

entreaty begging, pleading request – *Brokeback* (sl.) (Buckliger) – *jerk* [dʒɜːk] short quick movement – *moth* insect flying at night and attracted by lights (Motte) – *socket* an opening into which s.th. fits (here: Augenhöhle) – *trot* movement between walk and gallop; quick walk – *swamphaunt* (dial.) person that haunts the swamp; marsh ghost – *runt* small badly-developed person („lächerlicher Zwerg") – *to throw a fit* to have a sudden attack of uncontrolled temper – *cuff* light blow – *forlorn* [fəˈlɔːn] lonely and sad – *itch* a strong desire – *crossly* angrily – *rash* not thinking enough of the results

There were times when Miss Amelia seemed to go into a sort of trance. And the cause of these trances was usually known and understood. For Miss Amelia was a fine doctor, and did not grind up swamp roots and other untried ingredients and give them to the first patient who came along; whenever she invented a new medicine she always tried it out first on herself. She would swallow an enormous dose and spend the following day walking thoughtfully back and forth from the café to the brick privy. Often, when there was a sudden keen gripe, she would stand quite still, her queer eyes staring down at the ground and her fists clenched; she was trying to decide which organ was being worked upon, and what misery the new medicine might be most likely to cure. And now as she watched the hunchback and Marvin Macy, her face wore this same expression, tense with reckoning some inward pain, although she had taken no new medicine that day.

"That will learn you, Brokeback," said Marvin Macy.

Henry Macy pushed back his limp whitish hair from his forehead and coughed nervously. Stumpy MacPhail and Merlie Ryan shuffled their feet, and the children and black people on the outskirts of the property made not a sound. Marvin Macy folded the knife he had been honing, and after looking about him fearlessly he swaggered out of the yard. The embers in the pit were turning to gray feathery ashes and it was now quite dark.

XII That was the way Marvin Macy came back from the penitentiary. Not a living soul in all the town was glad to see him. Even Mrs. Mary Hale, who was a good woman and had raised him with love and care – at the first sight of him even this old foster mother dropped the skillet she was holding and burst into tears. But nothing could faze that Marvin Macy. He sat on the back steps of the Hale house, lazily picking his guitar, and when the supper was ready, he pushed the children of the household out of the way and served himself a big meal, although there had been barely enough hoecakes

keen sharp – *gripe* a sudden pressure or pain – *to clench* to close tightly – *that will learn you* (sl.) that will teach you – *embers* red-hot pieces of wood or coal in a fire that is no longer aflame – *skillet* (AE) frying pan – *to faze* (coll.) to surprise s.o. so much as to prevent speech or action – *hoecakes* a thin bread made of cornmeal

and white meat to go round. After eating he settled himself in the best and warmest sleeping place in the front room and was untroubled by dreams.

Miss Amelia did not open the café that night. She locked the doors and all the windows very carefully, nothing was seen of her and Cousin Lymon, and a lamp burned in her room all the night long.

Marvin Macy brought with him bad fortune, right from the first, as could be expected. The next day the weather turned suddenly, and it became hot. Even in the early morning there was a sticky sultriness in the atmosphere, the wind carried the rotten smell of the swamp, and delicate shrill mosquitoes webbed the green millpond. It was unseasonable, worse than August, and much damage was done. For nearly everyone in the county who owned a hog had copied Miss Amelia and slaughtered the day before. And what sausage could keep in such weather as this? After a few days there was everywhere the smell of slowly spoiling meat, and an atmosphere of dreary waste. Worse yet, a family reunion near the Forks Falls highway ate pork roast and died, every one of them. It was plain that their hog had been infected – and who could tell whether the rest of the meat was safe or not? People were torn between the longing for the good taste of pork, and the fear of death. It was a time of waste and confusion.

The cause of all this, Marvin Macy, had no shame in him. He was seen everywhere. During work hours he loafed about the mill, looking in at the windows, and on Sundays he dressed in his red shirt and paraded up and down the road with his guitar. He was still handsome – with his brown hair, his red lips, and his broad strong shoulders; but the evil in him was now too famous for his good looks to get him anywhere. And this evil was not measured only by the actual sins he had committed. True, he had robbed those filling stations. And before that he had ruined the tenderest girls in the county, and laughed about it. Any number of wicked things could be listed against him, but quite apart from these crimes there was about him a secret meanness that clung to him almost like a smell. Another thing

bad fortune an evil influence – *sticky* (coll.) hot and humid – *sultriness* hot weather with air which is hard to breathe (Schwüle) – *rotten* gone bad; nasty – *to web* to make a network by weaving threads together – *waste* unusable matter – *meanness* lack of decency; bad temper – *to cling to* to stick firmly to

– he never sweated, not even in August, and that surely is a sign worth pondering over.

Now it seemed to the town that he was more dangerous than he had ever been before, as in the penitentiary in Atlanta he must have learned the method of laying charms. Otherwise how could his effect on Cousin Lymon be explained? For since first setting eyes on Marvin Macy the hunchback was possessed by an unnatural spirit. Every minute he wanted to be following along behind this jailbird, and he was full of silly schemes to attract attention to himself. Still Marvin Macy either treated him hatefully or failed to notice him at all. Sometimes the hunchback would give up, perch himself on the banister of the front porch much as a sick bird huddles on a telephone wire, and grieve publicly.

"But why?" Miss Amelia would ask, staring at him with her crossed, gray eyes, and her fists closed tight.

"Oh, Marvin Macy," groaned the hunchback, and the sound of the name was enough to upset the rhythm of his sobs so that he hiccuped. "He has been to Atlanta."

Miss Amelia would shake her head and her face was dark and hardened. To begin with she had no patience with any traveling; those who had made the trip to Atlanta or traveled fifty miles from home to see the ocean – those restless people she despised. "Going to Atlanta does no credit to him."

"He has been to the penitentiary," said the hunchback, miserable with longing.

How are you going to argue against such envies as these? In her perplexity Miss Amelia did not herself sound any too sure of what she was saying. "Been to the penitentiary, Cousin Lymon? Why, a trip like that is no travel to brag about."

During these weeks Miss Amelia was closely watched by everyone. She went about absent-mindedly, her face remote as though she

to lay charms to exercise magic power – *to perch* to go into a position of rest (usually of a bird) – *to huddle* to draw or hunch o.s. up as from cold – *to groan* to say s.th. with a sound expressing pain – *to hiccup* ['hɪkʌp] to have a movement in one's chest which causes one to make a sudden sharp sound (einen Schluckauf haben) – *envy* ['envɪ] resentful dislike of s.o. who has s.th. one desires – *remote* far away

had lapsed into one of her gripe trances. For some reason, after the day of Marvin Macy's arrival, she put aside her overalls and wore always the red dress she had before this time reserved for Sundays, funerals, and sessions of the court. Then as the weeks passed she began to take some steps to clear up the situation. But her efforts were hard to understand. If it hurt her to see Cousin Lymon follow Marvin Macy about the town, why did she not make the issues clear once and for all, and tell the hunchback that if he had dealings with Marvin Macy she would turn him off the premises? That would have been simple, and Cousin Lymon would have had to submit to her, or else face the sorry business of finding himself loose in the world. But Miss Amelia seemed to have lost her will; for the first time in her life she hesitated as to just what course to pursue. And, like most people in such a position of uncertainty, she did the worst thing possible – she began following several courses at once, all of them contrary to each other.

The café was opened every night as usual, and, strangely enough, when Marvin Macy came swaggering through the door, with the hunchback at his heels, she did not turn him out. She even gave him free drinks and smiled at him in a wild, crooked way. At the same time she set a terrible trap for him out in the swamp that surely would have killed him if he had got caught. She let Cousin Lymon invite him to Sunday dinner, and then tried to trip him up as he went down the steps. She began a great campaign of pleasure for Cousin Lymon – making exhausting trips to various spectacles being held in distant places, driving the automobile thirty miles to a Chautauqua, taking him to Forks Falls to watch a parade. All in all it was a distracting time for Miss Amelia. In the opinion of most people she was well on her way in the climb up fools' hill, and everyone waited to see how it would all turn out.

The weather turned cold again, the winter was upon the town, and night came before the last shift in the mill was done. Children kept

to lapse into to slip into (a specified state) – *to submit to* to give in to – *trap* stratagem to trick an unsuspecting person (Falle) – *to trip up* to make s.o. fall by catching his foot – *Chautauqua* [ʃəˈtɔːkwə] an educational and recreational assembly with a programme of lectures or concerts – *to distract* to draw the mind away in another direction

on all their garments when they slept, and women raised the backs of their skirts to toast themselves dreamily at the fire. After it rained, the mud in the road made hard frozen ruts, there were faint flickers of lamplight from the windows of the houses, the peach trees were scrawny and bare. In the dark, silent nights of winter-time the café was the warm center point of the town, the lights shining so brightly that they could be seen a quarter of a mile away. The great iron stove at the back of the room roared, crackled, and turned red. Miss Amelia had made red curtains for the windows, and from a salesman who passed through the town she bought a great bunch of paper roses that looked very real.

But it was not only the warmth, the decorations, and the brightness, that made the café what it was. There is a deeper reason why the café was so precious to this town. And this deeper reason has to do with a certain pride that had not hitherto been known in these parts. To understand this new pride the cheapness of human life must be kept in mind. There were always plenty of people clustered around a mill – but it was seldom that every family had enough meal, garments, and fat back to go the rounds. Life could become one long dim scramble just to get the things needed to keep alive. And the confusing point is this: All useful things have a price, and are bought only with money, as that is the way the world is run. You know without having to reason about it the price of a bale of cotton, or a quart of molasses. But no value has been put on human life; it is given to us free and taken without being paid for. What is it worth? If you look around, at times the value may seem to be little or nothing at all. Often after you have sweated and tried and things are not better for you, there comes a feeling deep down in the soul that you are not worth much.

But the new pride that the café brought to this town had an effect on almost everyone, even the children. For in order to come to the café you did not have to buy the dinner, or a portion of liquor. There were cold bottled drinks for a nickel. And if you could not even

garments clothes – *scrawny* very thin – *dim* somewhat dark – *scramble* a disorderly struggle, as for s.th. prized – *bale* a large bundle compressed and bound – *molasses* [–'––] a thick brown syrup produced during the refining of sugar or from sorghum

afford that, Miss Amelia had a drink called Cherry Juice which sold for a penny a glass, and was pink-colored and very sweet. Almost everyone, with the exception of Reverend T. M. Willin, came to the café at least once during the week. Children love to sleep in houses other than their own, and to eat at a neighbor's table; on such occasions they behave themselves decently and are proud. The people in the town were likewise proud when sitting at the tables in the café. They washed before coming to Miss Amelia's, and scraped their feet very politely on the threshold as they entered the café. There, for a few hours at least, the deep bitter knowing that you are not worth much in this world could be laid low.

The café was a special benefit to bachelors, unfortunate people, and consumptives. And here it may be mentioned that there was some reason to suspect that Cousin Lymon was consumptive. The brightness of his gray eyes, his insistence, his talkativeness, and his cough – these were all signs. Besides, there is generally supposed to be some connection between a hunched spine and consumption. But whenever this subject had been mentioned to Miss Amelia she had become furious; she denied these symptoms with bitter vehemence, but on the sly she treated Cousin Lymon with hot chest platters, Kroup Kure, and such. Now this winter the hunchback's cough was worse, and sometimes even on cold days he would break out in a heavy sweat. But this did not prevent him from following along after Marvin Macy.

Early every morning he left the premises and went to the back door of Mrs. Hale's house, and waited and waited – as Marvin Macy was a lazy sleeper. He would stand there and call out softly. His voice was just like the voices of children who squat patiently over those tiny little holes in the ground where doodlebugs are thought to live, poking the hole with a broom straw, and calling plaintively: "Doodlebug, Doodlebug – fly away home. Mrs. Doodlebug, Mrs. Doodle-

to scrape to make clean by rubbing – *threshold* ['θreʃhəʊld] piece of wood fixed beneath the door (Schwelle) – *to lay low* (sl.) to keep hidden; to forget – *bachelor* unmarried man – *consumptive* having tuberculosis of the lungs – *spine* backbone – *chest platter* a pad or covering, as of flannel, for the chest – *to squat* to sit on one's heels, to crouch near to the ground – *doodlebug* larva of ant lion (Larve des Ameisenlöwen) – *plaintively* sounding sad; sorrowful

bug. Come out, come out. Your house is on fire and all your children are burning up." In just such a voice – at once sad, luring, and resigned – would the hunchback call Marvin Macy's name each morning. Then when Marvin Macy came out for the day, he would trail him about the town, and sometimes they would be gone for hours together out in the swamp.

And Miss Amelia continued to do the worst thing possible: that is, to try to follow several courses at once. When Cousin Lymon left the house she did not call him back, but only stood in the middle of the road and watched lonesomely until he was out of sight. Nearly every day Marvin Macy turned up with Cousin Lymon at dinnertime, and ate at her table. Miss Amelia opened the pear preserves, and the table was well-set with ham or chicken, great bowls of hominy grits, and winter peas. It is true that on one occasion Miss Amelia tried to poison Marvin Macy – but there was a mistake, the plates were confused, and it was she herself who got the poisoned dish. This she quickly realized by the slight bitterness of the food, and that day she ate no dinner. She sat tilted back in her chair, feeling her muscle, and looking at Marvin Macy.

Every night Marvin Macy came to the café and settled himself at the best and largest table, the one in the center of the room. Cousin Lymon brought him liquor, for which he did not pay a cent. Marvin Macy brushed the hunchback aside as if he were a swamp mosquito, and not only did he show no gratitude for these favors, but if the hunchback got in his way he would cuff him with the back of his hand, or say: "Out of my way, Brokeback – I'll snatch you baldheaded." When this happened Miss Amelia would come out from behind her counter and approach Marvin Macy very slowly, her fists clenched, her peculiar red dress hanging awkwardly around her bony knees. Marvin Macy would also clench his fists and they would walk slowly and meaningfully around each other. But, although everyone watched breathlessly, nothing ever came of it. The time for the fight was not yet ready.

There is one particular reason why this winter is remembered and still talked about. A great thing happened. People woke up on the

to lure to attract and tempt – *hominy grits* dry corn coarsely ground and boiled for food

second of January and found the whole world about them altogether changed. Little ignorant children looked out of the windows, and they were so puzzled that they began to cry. Old people harked back and could remember nothing in these parts to equal the phenomenon. For in the night it had snowed. In the dark hours after midnight the dim flakes started falling softly on the town. By dawn the ground was covered, and the strange snow banked the ruby windows of the church, and whitened the roofs of the houses. The snow gave the town a drawn, bleak look. The two-room houses near the mill were dirty, crooked, and seemed about to collapse, and somehow everything was dark and shrunken. But the snow itself – there was a beauty about it few people around here had ever known before. The snow was not white, as Northerners had pictured it to be; in the snow there were soft colors of blue and silver, the sky was a gentle shining gray. And the dreamy quietness of falling snow – when had the town been so silent?

People reacted to the snowfall in various ways. Miss Amelia, on looking out of her window, thoughtfully wiggled the toes of her bare foot, gathered close to her neck the collar of her nightgown. She stood there for some time, then commenced to draw the shutters and lock every window on the premises. She closed the place completely, lighted the lamps, and sat solemnly over her bowl of grits. The reason for this was not that Miss Amelia feared the snowfall. It was simply that she was unable to form an immediate opinion of this new event, and unless she knew exactly and definitely what she thought of a matter (which was nearly always the case) she preferred to ignore it. Snow had never fallen in this county in her lifetime, and she had never thought about it one way or the other. But if she admitted this snowfall she would have to come to some decision, and in those days there was enough distraction in her life as it was already. So she poked about the gloomy, lamplighted house and pretended that nothing had happened. Cousin Lymon, on the contrary, chased around in the wildest excitement, and when Miss Amelia turned her back to dish him some breakfast he slipped out of the door.

to hark back (arch.) to go back in thought – *drawn* tired – *bleak* (here) exposed to wind and cold – *to commence* to start – *distraction* s.th. that holds the attention – *to pretend* to claim falsely; to make believe

Marvin Macy laid claim to the snowfall. He said that he knew snow, had seen it in Atlanta, and from the way he walked about the town that day it was as though he owned every flake. He sneered at the little children who crept timidly out of the houses and scooped up handfuls of snow to taste. Reverend Willin hurried down the road with a furious face, as he was thinking deeply and trying to weave the snow into his Sunday sermon. Most people were humble and glad about this marvel; they spoke in hushed voices and said "thank you" and "please" more than was necessary. A few weak characters, of course, were demoralized and got drunk – but they were not numerous. To everyone this was an occasion and many counted their money and planned to go to the café that night.

Cousin Lymon followed Marvin Macy about all day, seconding his claim to the snow. He marveled that snow did not fall as does rain, and stared up at the dreamy, gently falling flakes until he stumbled from dizziness. And the pride he took on himself, basking in the glory of Marvin Macy – it was such that many people could not resist calling out to him: "'Oho,' said the fly on the chariot wheel. 'What a dust we do raise.'"

Miss Amelia did not intend to serve dinner. But when, at six o'clock, there was the sound of footsteps on the porch she opened the front door cautiously. It was Henry Ford Crimp, and though there was no food, she let him sit at a table and served him a drink. Others came. The evening was blue, bitter, and though the snow fell no longer there was a wind from the pine trees that swept up delicate flurries from the ground. Cousin Lymon did not come until after dark, with him Marvin Macy, and he carried his tin suitcase and his guitar.

"So you mean to travel?" said Miss Amelia quickly.

Marvin Macy warmed himself at the stove. Then he settled down at his table and carefully sharpened a little stick. He picked his teeth,

to sneer at to express contempt – *to scoop up* to gather up; to collect – *to weave into* (here) to work details of s.th. into; to introduce into – *sermon* talk given by a priest or minister in church – *humble* not proud – *marvel* a wonderful thing – *hushed* quiet – *to second* ['sekənd] to give support to – *to stumble* to walk in an unsteady manner – *dizziness* feeling of unsteadiness (Benommenheit) – *chariot* (arch.) a light, fourwheeled carriage used for pleasure or on state occasions – *flurry* a gust of snow

frequently taking the stick out of his mouth to look at the end and wipe it on the sleeve of his coat. He did not bother to answer.

The hunchback looked at Miss Amelia, who was behind the counter. His face was not in the least beseeching; he seemed quite sure of himself. He folded his hands behind his back and perked up his ears confidently. His cheeks were red, his eyes shining, and his clothes were soggy wet. "Marvin Macy is going to visit a spell with us," he said.

Miss Amelia made no protest. She only came out from behind the counter and hovered over the stove, as though the news had made her suddenly cold. She did not warm her backside modestly, lifting her skirt only an inch or so, as do most women when in public. There was not a grain of modesty about Miss Amelia, and she frequently seemed to forget altogether that there were men in the room. Now as she stood warming herself, her red dress was pulled up quite high in the back so that a piece of her strong, hairy thigh could be seen by anyone who cared to look at it. Her head was turned to one side, and she had begun talking with herself, nodding and wrinkling her forehead, and there was the tone of accusation and reproach in her voice although the words were not plain. Meanwhile, the hunchback and Marvin Macy had gone upstairs – up to the parlor with the pampas grass and the two sewing machines, to the private rooms where Miss Amelia had lived the whole of her life. Down in the café you could hear them bumping around, unpacking Marvin Macy, and getting him settled.

That is the way Marvin Macy crowded into Miss Amelia's home. At first Cousin Lymon, who had given Marvin Macy his own room, slept on the sofa in the parlor. But the snowfall had a bad effect on him; he caught a cold that turned into a winter quinsy, so Miss Amelia gave up her bed to him. The sofa in the parlor was much too short for her, her feet lapped over the edges, and often she rolled off onto the floor. Perhaps it was this lack of sleep that clouded her wits;

to beseech to ask for earnestly; to beg for – *to perk up* to raise (usually in order to show interest) – *soggy* soaked, wet – *a spell* (here) a while – *a grain* a (tiny) bit – *thigh* part of the leg between the knee and the hip – *to wrinkle* ['rɪnkəl] to cause to form into lines and folds

everything she tried to do against Marvin Macy rebounded on herself. She got caught in her own tricks, and found herself in many pitiful positions. But still she did not put Marvin Macy off the premises, as she was afraid that she would be left alone. Once you have lived with another, it is a great torture to have to live alone. The silence of a firelit room when suddenly the clock stops ticking, the nervous shadows in an empty house – it is better to take in your mortal enemy than face the terror of living alone.

The snow did not last. The sun came out and within two days the town was just as it had always been before. Miss Amelia did not open her house until every flake had melted. Then she had a big house cleaning and aired everything out in the sun. But before that, the very first thing she did on going out again into her yard, was to tie a rope to the largest branch of the chinaberry tree. At the end of the rope she tied a crocus sack tightly stuffed with sand. This was the punching bag she made for herself and from that day on she would box with it out in her yard every morning. Already she was a fine fighter – a little heavy on her feet, but knowing all manner of mean holds and squeezes to make up for this.

Miss Amelia, as has been mentioned, measured six feet two inches in height. Marvin Macy was one inch shorter. In weight they were about even – both of them weighing close to a hundred and sixty pounds. Marvin Macy had the advantage in slyness of movement, and in toughness of chest. In fact from the outward point of view the odds were altogether in his favor. Yet almost everybody in the town was betting on Miss Amelia; scarcely a person would put up money on Marvin Macy. The town remembered the great fight between Miss Amelia and a Fork Falls lawyer who had tried to cheat her. He had been a huge strapping fellow, but he was left three-quarters dead when she had finished with him. And it was not only her talent as a boxer that had impressed everyone – she could demoralize her enemy by making terrifying faces and fierce noises, so that even the spectators were sometimes cowed. She was brave, she practiced faithfully

chinaberry tree an Asiatic tree of the mahogany family – *crocus* an orange-yellow colour – *strapping* (coll.) robust – *fierce* violent – *to cow s.o.* to make timid by filling with fear; to intimidate

with her punching bag, and in this case she was clearly in the right. So people had confidence in her, and they waited. Of course there was no set date for this fight. There were just the signs that were too plain to be overlooked.

During these times the hunchback strutted around with a pleased little pinched-up face. In many delicate and clever ways he stirred up trouble between them. He was constantly plucking at Marvin Macy's trouser leg to draw attention to himself. Sometimes he followed in Miss Amelia's footsteps – but these days it was only in order to imitate her awkward long-legged walk; he crossed his eyes and aped her gestures in a way that made her appear to be a freak. There was something so terrible about this that even the silliest customers of the café, such as Merlie Ryan, did not laugh. Only Marvin Macy drew up the left corner of his mouth and chuckled. Miss Amelia, when this happened, would be divided between two emotions. She would look at the hunchback with a lost, dismal reproach – then turn toward Marvin Macy with her teeth clamped.

"Bust a gut!" she would say bitterly.

And Marvin Macy, most likely, would pick up the guitar from the floor beside his chair. His voice was wet and slimy, as he always had too much spit in his mouth. And the tunes he sang glided slowly from his throat like eels. His strong fingers picked the strings with dainty skill, and everything he sang both lured and exasperated. This was usually more than Miss Amelia could stand.

"Bust a gut!" she would repeat, in a shout.

But always Marvin Macy had the answer ready for her. He would cover the strings to silence the quivering leftover tones, and reply with slow, sure insolence.

"Everything you holler at me bounces back on yourself. Yah! Yah!"

Miss Amelia would have to stand there helpless, as no one has ever invented a way out of this trap. She could not shout out abuse that

pinched-up thin and tired-looking – *to pluck at* to pull sharply – *freak* an abnormal person – *dismal* depressed; miserable – *to bust* to burst or break – *eel* fish that are shaped like snakes, long and slippery – *insolence* disrespect

would bounce back on herself. He had the best of her, there was nothing she could do.

So things went on like this. What happened between the three of them during the nights in the rooms upstairs nobody knows. But the café became more and more crowded every night. A new table had to be brought in. Even the Hermit, the crazy man named Rainer Smith, who took to the swamps years ago, heard something of the situation and came one night to look in at the window and brood over the gathering in the bright café. And the climax each evening was the time when Miss Amelia and Marvin Macy doubled their fists, squared up, and glared at each other. Usually this did not happen after any especial argument, but it seemed to come about mysteriously, by means of some instinct on the part of both of them. At these times the café would become so quiet that you could hear the bouquet of paper roses rustling in the draft. And each night they held this fighting stance a little longer than the night before.

XIII The fight took place on Ground Hog Day, which is the second of February. The weather was favorable, being neither rainy nor sunny, and with a neutral temperature. There were several signs that this was the appointed day, and by ten o'clock the news spread all over the county. Early in the morning Miss Amelia went out and cut down her punching bag. Marvin Macy sat on the back step with a tin can of hog fat between his knees and carefully greased his arms and his legs. A hawk with a bloody breast flew over the town and circled twice around the property of Miss Amelia. The tables in the café were moved out to the back porch, so that the whole big room was cleared for the fight. There was every sign. Both Miss Amelia and Marvin Macy ate four helpings of half-raw roast for dinner, and then lay down in the afternoon to store up strength. Marvin Macy rested in the big room upstairs, while Miss Amelia stretched herself out on the bench in her office. It was plain from her white stiff face what a torment it was for her to be lying still and doing nothing, but she lay

hermit a person who lives in a lonely spot (for religious motives) – *to brood over* to think about in a morbid way – *draft* a current of air – *ground-hog* woodchuck (Murmeltier) – *to appoint* to set a date – *hawk* falcon-like bird

there quiet as a corpse with her eyes closed and her hands crossed on her chest.

Cousin Lymon had a restless day, and his little face was drawn and tightened with excitement. He put himself up a lunch, and set out to find the ground hog – within an hour he returned, the lunch eaten, and said that the ground hog had seen his shadow and there was to be bad weather ahead. Then, as Miss Amelia and Marvin Macy were both resting to gather strength, and he was left to himself, it occurred to him that he might as well paint the front porch. The house had not been painted for years – in fact, God knows if it had ever been painted at all. Cousin Lymon scrambled around, and soon he had painted half the floor of the porch a gay bright green. It was a loblolly job, and he smeared himself all over. Typically enough he did not even finish the floor, but changed over to the walls, painting as high as he could reach and then standing on a crate to get up a foot higher. When the paint ran out, the right side of the floor was bright green and there was a jagged portion of wall that had been painted. Cousin Lymon left it at that.

There was something childish about his satisfaction with his painting. And in this respect a curious fact should be mentioned. No one in the town, not even Miss Amelia, had any idea how old the hunchback was. Some maintained that when he came to town he was about twelve years old, still a child – others were certain that he was well past forty. His eyes were blue and steady as a child's but there were lavender crêpy shadows beneath these blue eyes that hinted of age. It was impossible to guess his age by his hunched queer body. And even his teeth gave no clue – they were all still in his head (two were broken from cracking a pecan), but he had stained them with so much sweet snuff that it was impossible to decide whether they were old teeth or young teeth. When questioned directly about his age the hunchback professed to know absolutely nothing – he had no idea how long he had been on the earth, whether for ten years or a hundred! So his age remained a puzzle.

corpse a dead body – *loblolly* (dial.) disorderly – *jagged* ['dʒægɪd] having a rough, uneven edge – *crêpy* ['kreɪpɪ] the quality of thin, crinkled cloth (krepp-artig) – *pecan* [pɪ'kæn] an olive-shaped edible nut – *to profess* [–'–] to affirm

Cousin Lymon finished his painting at five-thirty o'clock in the afternoon. The day had turned colder and there was a wet taste in the air. The wind came up from the pinewoods, rattling windows, blowing an old newspaper down the road until at last it caught upon a thorn tree. People began to come in from the country; packed automobiles that bristled with the poked-out heads of children, wagons drawn by old mules who seemed to smile in a weary, sour way and plodded along with their tired eyes half-closed. Three young boys came from Society City. All three of them wore yellow rayon shirts and caps put on backward – they were as much alike as triplets, and could always be seen at cock fights and camp meetings. At six o'clock the mill whistle sounded the end of the day's shift and the crowd was complete. Naturally, among the newcomers there were some riffraff, unknown characters, and so forth – but even so the gathering was quiet. A hush was on the town and the faces of people were strange in the fading light. Darkness hovered softly; for a moment the sky was a pale clear yellow against which the gables of the church stood out in dark and bare outline, then the sky died slowly and the darkness gathered into night.

Seven is a popular number, and especially it was a favorite with Miss Amelia. Seven swallows of water for hiccups, seven runs around the millpond for cricks in the neck, seven doses of Amelia Miracle Mover as a worm cure – her treatment nearly always hinged on this number. It is a number of mingled possibilities, and all who love mystery and charms set store by it. So the fight was to take place at seven o'clock. This was known to everyone, not by announcement or words, but understood in the unquestioning way that rain is understood, or an evil odor from the swamp. So before seven o'clock everyone gathered gravely around the property of Miss Amelia. The cleverest got into the café itself and stood lining the walls of the room. Others crowded onto the front porch, or took a stand in the yard.

thorn tree small tree or shrub bearing thorns – *to bristle* to be thickly packed – *to plod along* to move heavily and laboriously – *rayon* man-made material which can be made to look like silk, cotton, wool, etc. – *triplets* three children born at a single birth – *riffraff* disreputable, worthless people – *crick* stiffness and pain in a part of the body – *to hinge* (here) to depend on

Miss Amelia and Marvin Macy had not yet shown themselves. Miss Amelia, after resting all afternoon on the office bench, had gone upstairs. On the other hand Cousin Lymon was at your elbow every minute, threading his way through the crowd, snapping his fingers nervously, and batting his eyes. At one minute to seven o'clock he squirmed his way into the café and climbed up on the counter. All was very quiet.

It must have been arranged in some manner beforehand. For just at the stroke of seven Miss Amelia showed herself at the head of the stairs. At the same instant Marvin Macy appeared in front of the café and the crowd made way for him silently. They walked toward each other with no haste, their fists already gripped, and their eyes like the eyes of dreamers. Miss Amelia had changed her red dress for her old overalls, and they were rolled up to the kness. She was barefooted and she had an iron strengthband around her right wrist. Marvin Macy had also rolled his trouser legs – he was naked to the waist and heavily greased; he wore the heavy shoes that had been issued him when he left the penitentiary. Stumpy MacPhail stepped forward from the crowd and slapped their hip pockets with the palm of his right hand to make sure there would be no sudden knives. Then they were alone in the cleared center of the bright café.

There was no signal, but they both struck out simultaneously. Both blows landed on the chin, so that the heads of Miss Amelia and Marvin Macy bobbed back and they were left a little groggy. For a few seconds after the first blows they merely shuffled their feet around on the bare floor, experimenting with various positions, and making mock fists. Then, like wildcats, they were suddenly on each other. There was the sound of knocks, panting, and thumpings on the floor. They were so fast that it was hard to take in what was going on – but once Miss Amelia was hurled backward so that she staggered and almost fell, and another time Marvin Macy caught a knock on the shoulder that spun him around like a top. So the fight went on in this wild violent way with no sign of weakening on either side.

to bat one's eyes to close and open the eyes quickly — *to squirm* to twist and turn the body like a snake – *to bob back* to move back with short jerky motions – *mock* not real, imitation

During a struggle like this, when the enemies are as quick and strong as these two, it is worth-while to turn from the confusion of the fight itself and observe the spectators. The people had flattened back as close as possible against the walls. Stumpy MacPhail was in a corner, crouched over and with his fists tight in sympathy, making strange noises. Poor Merlie Ryan had his mouth so wide open that a fly buzzed into it, and was swallowed before Merlie realized what had happened. And Cousin Lymon – he was worth watching. The hunchback still stood on the counter, so that he was raised up above everyone else in the café. He had his hands on his hips, his big head thrust forward, and his little legs bent so that the knees jutted outward. The excitement had made him break out in a rash, and his pale mouth shivered.

Perhaps it was half an hour before the course of the fight shifted. Hundreds of blows had been exchanged, and there was still a deadlock. Then suddenly Marvin Macy managed to catch hold of Miss Amelia's left arm and pinion it behind her back. She struggled and got a grasp around his waist; the real fight was now begun. Wrestling is the natural way of fighting in this county – as boxing is too quick and requires much thinking and concentration. And now that Miss Amelia and Marvin were locked in a hold together the crowd came out of its daze and pressed in closer. For a while the fighters grappled muscle to muscle, their hipbones braced against each other. Backward and forward, from side to side, they swayed in this way. Marvin Macy still had not sweated, but Miss Amelia's overalls were drenched and so much sweat had trickled down her legs that she left wet footprints on the floor. Now the test had come, and in these moments of terrible effort, it was Miss Amelia who was the stronger. Marvin Macy was greased and slippery, tricky to grasp, but she was stronger. Gradually she bent him over backward, and inch by inch she forced him to the floor. It was a terrible thing to watch and their deep hoarse breaths were the only sound in the café.

to jut outward to stick out – *rash* an eruption of red spots on the skin – *deadlock* a standstill between opposing sides in a contest – *to pinion* to hold tight – *to wrestle* ['resl] to struggle hand to hand with an opponent – *daze* shock; bewilderment (Benommenheit) – *to brace* to press firmly – *to sway* to swing to and fro – *hoarse* sounding rough and husky

At last she had him down, and straddled; her strong big hands were on his throat.

But at that instant, just as the fight was won, a cry sounded in the café that caused a shrill bright shiver to run down the spine. And what took place has been a mystery ever since. The whole town was there to testify what happened, but there were those who doubted their own eyesight. For the counter on which Cousin Lymon stood was at least twelve feet from the fighters in the center of the café. Yet at the instant Miss Amelia grasped the throat of Marvin Macy the hunchback sprang forward and sailed through the air as though he had grown hawk wings. He landed on the broad strong back of Miss Amelia and clutched at her neck with his clawed little fingers.

The rest is confusion. Miss Amelia was beaten before the crowd could come to their senses. Because of the hunchback the fight was won by Marvin Macy, and at the end Miss Amelia lay sprawled on the floor, her arms flung outward and motionless. Marvin Macy stood over her, his face somewhat popeyed, but smiling his old half-mouthed smile. And the hunchback, he had suddenly disappeared. Perhaps he was frightened about what he had done, or maybe he was so delighted that he wanted to glory with himself alone – at any rate he slipped out of the café and crawled under the back steps. Someone poured water on Miss Amelia, and after a time she got up slowly and dragged herself into her office. Through the open door the crowd could see her sitting at her desk, her head in the crook of her arm, and she was sobbing with the last of her grating, winded breath. Once she gathered her right fist together and knock it three times on the top of her office desk, then her hand opened feebly and lay palm upward and still. Stumpy MacPhail stepped forward and closed the door.

The crowd was quiet, and one by one the people left the café. Mules were waked up and untied, automobiles cranked, and the three boys from Society City roamed off down the road on foot. This was not a fight to hash over and talk about afterward; people went home and pulled the covers up over their heads. The town was

popeyed having wide protruding eyes – *crook* bend or curve – *to grate* to make a rasping sound – *to hash over* (coll.) to discuss at length

dark, except for the premises of Miss Amelia, but every room was lighted there the whole night long.

Marvin Macy and the hunchback must have left the town an hour or so before daylight. And before they went away this is what they did:

They unlocked the private cabinet of curios and took everything in it.

They broke the mechanical piano.

They carved terrible words on the café tables.

They found the watch that opened in the back to show a picture of a waterfall and took that also.

They poured a gallon of sorghum syrup all over the kitchen floor and smashed the jars of preserves.

They went out in the swamp and completely wrecked the still, ruining the big new condenser and the cooler, and setting fire to the shack itself.

They fixed a dish of Miss Amelia's favorite food, grits with sausage, seasoned it with enough poison to kill off the county, and placed this dish temptingly on the café counter.

They did everything ruinous they could think of without actually breaking into the office where Miss Amelia stayed the night. Then they went off together, the two of them.

XIV That was how Miss Amelia was left alone in the town. The people would have helped her if they had known how, as people in this town will as often as not be kindly if they have a chance. Several housewives nosed around with brooms and offered to clear up the wreck. But Miss Amelia only looked at them with lost crossed eyes and shook her head. Stumpy MacPhail came in on the third day to buy a plug of Queenie tobacco, and Miss Amelia said the price was one dollar. Everything in the café had suddenly risen in price to be worth one dollar. And what sort of a café is that? Also, she changed very queerly as a doctor. In all the years before she had been much more popular than the Cheehaw doctor. She had never monkeyed with a patient's soul, taking away from him such real necessities as liquor, tobacco, and so forth. Once in a great while she might carefully warn a patient never to eat fried watermelon or some such dish it had never occurred to a person to want in the first place. Now all this wise doctoring was over. She told one-half of her patients that they were going to die outright, and to the remaining half she recommended cures so far-fetched and agonizing that no one in his right mind would consider them for a moment.

Miss Amelia let her hair grow ragged, and it was turning gray. Her face lengthened, and the great muscles of her body shrank until she was thin as old maids are thin when they go crazy. And those gray eyes – slowly day by day they were more crossed, and it was as though they sought each other out to exchange a little glance of grief and lonely recognition. She was not pleasant to listen to; her tongue had sharpened terribly.

When anyone mentioned the hunchback she would say only this: "Ho! If I could lay hand to him I would rip out his gizzard and throw it to the cat!" But it was not so much the words that were terrible, but the voice in which they were said. Her voice had lost its old vigor; there was none of the ring of vengeance it used to have when she would mention "that loom-fixer I was married to," or some other enemy. Her voice was broken, soft, and sad as the wheezy whine of the church pump-organ.

For three years she sat out on the front steps every night, alone and silent, looking down the road and waiting. But the hunchback never returned. There were rumors that Marvin Macy used him to climb into windows and steal, and other rumors that Marvin Macy had sold him into a side show. But both these reports were traced back to Merlie Ryan. Nothing true was ever heard of him. It was in the fourth year that Miss Amelia hired a Cheehaw carpenter and had him board up the premises, and there in those closed rooms she has remained ever since.

XV Yes, the town is dreary. On August afternoons the road is empty, white with dust, and the sky above is bright as glass. Nothing moves – there are no children's voices, only the hum of the mill. The peach trees seem to grow more crooked every summer, and the leaves are dull gray and of a sickly delicacy. The house of Miss Amelia leans so much to the right that it is now only a question

to agonize to cause great pain to – *vigor* vitality – *vengeance* severe harm done to s.o. as a punishment for harm he has done to o.s. (Rache) – *wheezy* characterized by a breathy sound, as in asthma – *whine* peevish, high-pitched, nasal sound, as in distress – *pump-organ* musical instrument (mit Blasebalg betriebenes Orgelpositiv)

of time when it will collapse completely, and people are careful not to walk around the yard. There is no good liquor to be bought in the town; the nearest still is eight miles away, and the liquor is such that those who drink it grow warts on their livers the size of goobers, and dream themselves into a dangerous inward world. There is absolutely nothing to do in the town. Walk around the millpond, stand kicking at a rotten stump, figure out what you can do with the old wagon wheel by the side of the road near the church. The soul rots with boredom. You might as well go down to the Forks Falls highway and listen to the chain gang.

XVI THE TWELVE MORTAL MEN

The Forks Falls highway is three miles from the town, and it is here the chain gang has been working. The road is of macadam, and the county decided to patch up the rough places and widen it at a certain dangerous place. The gang is made up of twelve men, all wearing black and white striped prison suits, and chained at the ankles. There is a guard, with a gun, his eyes drawn to red slits by the glare. The gang works all the day long, arriving huddled in the prison cart soon after daybreak, and being driven off again in the gray August twilight. All day there is the sound of the picks striking into the clay earth, hard sunlight, the smell of sweat. And every day there is music. One dark voice will start a phrase, half-sung, and like a question. And after a moment another voice will join in, soon the whole gang will be singing. The voices are dark in the golden glare, the music intricately blended, both somber and joyful. The music will swell until at last it seems that the sound does not come from the twelve men on the gang, but from the earth itself, or the wide sky. It is music that causes the heart to broaden and the listener to grow cold with ecstasy and fright. Then slowly the music will sink down until at last there remains one lonely voice, then a great hoarse breath, the sun, the sound of the picks in the silence.

And what kind of gang is this that can make such music? Just twelve mortal men, seven of them black and five of them white boys from this county. Just twelve mortal men who are together.

goober (dial.) a peanut – *macadam* [məˈkædəm] small broken stones, combined with tar, used in making roads – *pick* a heavy tool used for breaking up rock

Comprehension, Analysis, and Discussion

The following questions cover various fields of study and methodical skills of literary appreciation relating to the categories of setting, plot, character, point of view, theme, language, etc.

One possible classroom approach that allows for the principle of cursory reading is that of group work where several groups of pupils focus on a number of questions and then present and exchange their results. Of course, they must have read the text at home.

I

1. Describe the setting of Carson McCuller's short novel (time, place, atmosphere).
2. How do human beings relate to this environment?
3. Comment on the function of this setting.

II

1. What do the following sentences tell us about the overall structure of the novel: "The café has long since been closed, but it is still remembered. The place was not always a café. Miss Amelia inherited the building from her father, and it was a store ..."?
2. What do we learn about Miss Amelia Evans's personality and occupation?
3. Before "Cousin" Lymon Willis arrives, a few townspeople keep Amelia Evans company on her porch. Why is this important?
4. Describe Lymon Willis. Comment on his request and the way in which he presents it.
5. What role do Amelia's "fellow citizens" play during the stranger's initial conversation with her?
6. Do you share the implied narrator's opinion as to the importance of Miss Amelia's whisky?

III

1. Comment on Amelia's attitude towards the "strange" hunchback.
2. What do you think of the atmosphere that pervades the protagonist's home?

IV

1. Comment on the gradual spreading of the rumour. Try to group the townspeople with regard to their attitude towards the sensational story.
2. Elaborate on the relationship between the townspeople and Miss Amelia as presented at the beginning of this section.
3. What further information about Miss Amelia's character can be gathered from the description of her office?
4. How does McCullers succeed in building up suspense and creating a kind of climax in this section?
5. Evaluate the changes in Lymon's behaviour when he emerges from his retreat.
6. How do Lymon Willis and the townspeople get along with one another?
7. To what extent can one speak of a change in Amelia's attitude towards her customers? How is it brought about? Does it seem convincing?
8. What social consequences does the initial celebration have?

V

1. The sentences "Now time must pass. For the next four years are much alike." indicate McCullers' use of the time-lapse technique. Comment on the different effect of this mode of narration on the reader in comparison with the narrative mode of the preceding scene.
2. What is life for Lymon and Amelia like during those four years?

VI

1. McCullers first renders the opinions of the townspeople on the kind of love that exists between Lymon and Amelia. Summarize them.
2. There is a shift in the narrative mode within this section. What is its function?
3. The author then makes some general remarks about love. In what way are they important for the story?

VII

1. What structural aim does the flashback character of this section have?
2. What do we learn about Marvin Macy's growing up and adolescence?
3. Contrast Marvin's personality as it appears before and after his falling in love with Amelia. Do the changes seem convincing to you? To what extent can one speak of a recurring motif in the novel?
4. Summarize the description of the wedding ceremony and comment on it.
5. Describe, and comment on, Marvin's and Amelia's activities after their wedding. Why does the marriage remain unconsummated?
6. What happens to Marvin after he leaves the town? Can you explain this?
7. What is the function of the last paragraph of Section VII? What is the implied narrator's attitude? Where does the author come in?

VIII

1. Describe Miss Amelia's rooms.
2. What do we learn about the conversations between Miss Amelia and Cousin Lymon?
3. What does Amelia remember about her father? What kind of relationship did the two have?

IX

1. Comment on the atmosphere pervading the town and the café.
2. Why does Carson McCullers include a more detailed description of Amelia's treatment of a child in this section?
3. Lymon's personality, once again, appears in a different light. What do we learn about him?
4. How does Amelia react to Willis's antics?
5. Trace hints in this section that foreshadow complications and serve to build up suspense.
6. What is Amelia's reaction to the news of her former husband's being released from penitentiary on probation?

X

1. Compare the beginnings of Sections IX and X with regard to their respective presentation of atmosphere.
2. What is Miss Amelia doing during that "happy time" in autumn?
3. Comment on the description of the first meeting between Lymon and Marvin.
4. Lymon disobeys Amelia's orders by trespassing beyond her "boundary." To what extent may this be considered a foreshadowing of the outcome of the story?
5. How do the townspeople react to Marvin's return?

XI

1. Describe Miss Evans's reaction to seeing Marvin Macy and Lymon Willis standing close to each other.
2. How does Cousin Lymon usually succeed in calming Miss Amelia down? What does that prove about their relationship?
3. Comment on Lymon's attempt at getting to know Marvin Macy. How does the latter respond to his advances?
4. Does this section offer a solution as far as the pending conflict between Miss Evans and her legal husband is concerned? Give reasons.

XII

1. This section contains a number of illustrations of Marvin Macy's character. Summarize and evaluate them.
2. Can you accept the link – established by the implied narrator – between Macy's return to town and the "misfortune" that befalls it at the same time? What is the function of these coincidences?
3. What reason does Lymon give Amelia for being attracted to Marvin Macy?
4. What steps does Amelia take to "clear up the situation"? Why doesn't she act coherently?
5. How does the implied narrator account for the fact that "the café was so precious to this town"? Do you agree with the assumption about "the cheapness of human life"?
6. Try to recapitulate the steps by which Marvin Macy re-establishes himself in Miss Amelia's home.

7. What information does McCullers give in order to prepare the reader for the decisive fight between the two antagonists.

XIII

1. What further information is the reader given about Lymon Willis?
2. What character does the fight take on as a result of the fact that crowds of people from miles around come to watch it?
3. Which narrative elements serve to ritualize the fight?
4. Describe the various stages of the fight.
5. Summarize the reactions of the three principle characters and the spectators to the end and outcome of the fight.

XIV

1. To what extent does this section shed a positive light on the townspeople?
2. How does McCullers illustrate the disintegration of Amelia's personality?

XV

1. Comment on the structural significance of the statement, "Yes, the town is dreary."
2. What kind of microcosm does the "town" seem to be?

XVI

1. Comment on the activities of the chain gang.
2. What is the attitude of the implied narrator towards the twelve men in the chain gang?

Suggested Topics for General Study

1. Comment on the plot of the novel. Make a diagram of the most important parts and analyze their function within the whole.
2. To what extent are major and minor characters in the book convincingly drawn?
3. Interpret the "setting" in *The Ballad of the Sad Café* by commenting on its function and significance.
4. Select passages and sentences in the novel that reveal the implied narrator's ideas on the plot and content of the story.
5. What concept of writing as a creative process does McCullers develop in her essay "The Flowering Dream"? (cf. *Material for Further Study*, p. 84)
6. a) Comment on the distribution of static and dynamic elements.
   b) With this particular novel in mind, study L.D. Rubin's critical statement: "Carson McCullers' fiction, interesting though it was, seemed limited in its scope; it stopped short of the tragic, contenting itself with a poignant exploration of surfaces."
7. Compare the novel with another English or German ballad and say why you think Carson McCullers called her story a ballad.
8. Might an obvious lack in motivational depth be explained and excused by the fact that McCullers applied the term "ballad" to her short novel?
9. Examine Southern small-town life as presented in this short novel. Depict and evaluate the relationship between the individual (Miss Amelia; Marvin Macy; Lymon Willis) and society (the townspeople as a whole).
10. To what extent does the novel contain folk elements and traces of superstition? What role is assigned to the official (Baptist) church and to religious faith in general?
11. Trace the development of the themes of love and pain, guilt and retribution in the novel.
12. To what extent can the chain gang mentioned at the beginning of the book and described in greater detail at the end be considered an extended metaphor for what is narrated in the book?
13. Study the five critical sources on McCullers' work *(cf. Material for Further Study)* and list the positive and negative responses. What is your own opinion of this novel?

Material for Further Study

1. Carson McCullers on Writing as a Creative Process and on the Significance of the South

Spiritual isolation is the basis of most of my themes. My first book was concerned with this, almost entirely, and all of my books since, in one way or another. Love, and especially love of a person who is incapable of returning or receiving it, is at the heart of my selection of grotesque figures to write about – people whose physical incapacity is a symbol of their spiritual incapacity to love or receive love – their spiritual isolation ...

The dimensions of a work of art are seldom realized by the author until the work is accomplished. It is like a flowering dream. Ideas grow, budding silently, and there are a thousand illuminations coming day by day as the work progresses. A seed grows in writing as in nature. The seed of the idea is developed by both labour and the unconscious, and the struggle that goes on between them.

I understand only particles. I understand the characters but the novel itself is not in focus. The focus comes at random moments which no one can understand, least of all the author. For me, they usually follow great effort. To me, these illuminations are the grace of labour. All of my work has happened this way. It is at once the hazard and the beauty that a writer has to depend on such illuminations. After months of confusion and labour, when the idea has flowered, the collusion is Divine. It always comes from the subconscious and cannot be controlled ...

A writer's main asset is intuition; too many facts impede intuition. A writer needs to know so many things, but there are so many things he doesn't need to know – he needs to know human things even if they aren't "wholesome", as they call it ...

I become the characters I write about. I am so immersed in them that their motives are my own. When I write about a thief, I become one; when I write about Captain Penderton, I become a homosexual man; when I write about a deaf mute, I become dumb during the time of the story. I become the characters I write about and I bless the Latin poet Terence who said, "Nothing human is alien to me."

People ask me why I don't go back to the South more often. But the South is a very emotional experience for me, fraught with all the memories of my childhood. When I go back South I always get into arguments, so that a visit to Columbus in Georgia is a stirring up of love and antagonism. The locale of my books might always be Southern, and the South always my homeland. I love the voices of Negroes – like brown rivers. I feel that in the short trips when I do go to the South, in my own memory and in the newspaper articles, I still have my own reality.

Many authors find it hard to write about new environments that they did not know in childhood. The voices reheard from childhood have a truer pitch. And the foliage – the trees of childhood – are remembered more exactly. When I work from within a different locale from the South, I have to wonder what time the flowers are in bloom – and what flowers? I hardly let characters speak unless they are Southern. Wolfe wrote brilliantly of Brooklyn, but more brilliantly of the Southern cadence and ways of speech. This is particularly true of Southern writers because it is not only their speech and foliage, but their entire culture – which makes it a homeland within a homeland. No matter what the politics, the degree or non-degree of liberalism in a Southern writer, he is still bound to this peculiar regionalism of language and voices and foliage and memory.

Few Southern writers are truly cosmopolitan. When Faulkner writes about the R.A.F. and France, he is somewhat not convincing – while I'm convinced in almost every line about Yoknapatapha County. Indeed, to me *The Sound and the Fury* is probably the greatest American novel. It has an authenticity, a grandeur and, most of all, a tenderness that stems from the combination of reality and the dream that is the divine collusion . . .

The passionate, individual love – the old Tristan-Isolde love, the Eros love – is inferior to the love of God, to fellowship, to the love of Agape – the Greek god of the feast, the God of brotherly love – and of man. This is what I tried to show in *The Ballad of the Sad Café* in the strange love of Miss Amelia for the little hunchback, Cousin Lymon.

The writer's work is predicated not only on his personality but by the region in which he was born. I wonder sometimes if what they call the "Gothic" school of Southern writing, in which the grotesque is paralleled with the sublime, is not due largely to the cheapness of human life in the South. The Russians are like the Southern writers in that respect. In my childhood, the South was almost a feudal society. But the South is complicated by the racial problem more severely than the Russian society. To many a poor Southerner, the only pride that he has is the fact that he is white, and when one's self-pride is so pitiably debased, how can one learn to love? (1959)

(Carson McCullers, "The Flowering Dream", in *The Mortgaged Heart,* Harmondsworth: Penguin, 1975, pp. 280–87).

2. Critical Opinions on Carson McCullers and her Work

But the best work of Carson McCullers may be *The Ballad of the Sad Café* (1951), in which Amazon-like Miss Amelia, her hunchback cousin Lymon, and her husband-for-a-night, evil Marvin Macy, play out the ballad of loneliness and maimed desire and love condemned to loss, while a chain gang suffers, sings, endures. In the small dreary town, behind shutters, the face of Miss Amelia will still appear, a face "sexless and white, with two gray crossed eyes which are turned inward so sharply that they seem to be exchanging with each other one long secret gaze of grief."

(Ihab Hassan, *Contemporary American Literature 1945–1972. An Introduction,* New York: Frederick Ungar Publishing Co., 1974, pp. 68/69.)

McCuller's myth-making power was to fit this obsessive loneliness, this sense of total weakness before real earthly damnation, into the Southern climate, the town in summer, the doldrums of children with nowhere to go. She made different lacks [i.e. deficiencies] equal illuminations of the system of life in a Southern town. The bareness, vacancy, inertia seem to come out of the weather; the emotions of solitude flourish crazily in the parched streets; even McCullers's concentration on absolute clarity of style suggests the same still, depressed, vacant atmosphere, produces distinctness as a tragic effect ...

McCullers had the intuition that human beings could be psychic states so absolute and self-contained that they repelled each other sexually ... Though she converted this sense of some deep personal unnaturalness into brilliant "atmosphere" ... the demon of self-damnation, of being utterly locked up, sexually limited, was a subject that fascinated her but which she objectified, as comedy, only once –

in *The Ballad of the Sad Café* ... But in the *Ballad,* emotionally the most detached of her fictions, the distrust of sex which runs all through her work expresses itself as a folk tale in which the characters are mostly legends, unnatural and against nature. Everything is seen as a fable; there is nothing of that pervasive cry for sympathy which fills up *The Heart is a Lonely Hunter* like a gas, numbing us ...

Miss Amelia shows what a woman past love can do with her energy. At the end, her exasperated ex-husband, when released from prison, tries to bring her back to his world of passion. She prefers to be a magician – or author – in perfect control. She fights it out with him in a long-drawn-out battle of comic fisticuffs that betrays her desire to lose and her inability to get any profit out of her strength except the solitude which feeds it.

(Alfred Kazin, *Bright Book of Life, American Novelists and Storytellers from Hemingway to Mailer,* Boston-Toronto: Little, Brown and Co., 1971, pp. 52–54.)

Auch in der zeitgenössischen Literatur, so kahl und radikal sie manchmal erscheint, existieren Märchen von grausamer Schönheit, sie sterben nicht aus. Nur sind sie heute in geräumigen Kontinenten eher zu Hause als auf dem besetzten Schachbrett Europas. Es ist, als müsse die literarische Wiederentdeckung des Märchenhaften Anlauf nehmen über weite Strecken. Eines scheint das Legendäre vor allem zu begünstigen: ein Klima, das die Natur der Beherrschung durch die Technik mit Urgewalt entzieht.

Nicht von ungefähr haben die Südstaaten Amerikas immer wieder literarische Eruptionen hervorgebracht. Allein unter Schriftstellern, deren Namen heute Weltruhm bedeuten, findet man dort mehr als ein halbes Dutzend beheimatet: Autoren wie William Faulkner, Tennessee Williams, Truman Capote. Das Werk von Thomas Wolfe hat dort seinen Ursprung nicht weniger als das von Robert Penn Warren, Erskine Caldwell oder Katherine Anne Porter. Aus dem amerikanischen Süden kam auch jenes Mädchen, das vor einem Vierteljahrhundert die literarische Welt durch ein Erstlingswerk von erlesener Seltsamkeit verblüffte. Was sie anstimmte von neuem, auf vorher nicht dagewesene Weise, war das Fabelhafte, das traurige Märchen des Südens. Seit damals gehört diese Autorin zu den wenigen Unverwechselbaren. Ihr Name ist Carson McCullers.

Sich einlassen auf dieses Werk und dieses Leben heißt eintreten in das Kraftfeld einer außerordentlichen Persönlichkeit. Ihr Dasein selbst ist inzwischen Legende geworden. Einsam, vermögend, für immer krank, lebte sie in der Nähe New Yorks – durchdringend ähnlich einer Figur aus einem ihrer Romane. Carson McCullers, hochgeschätzt unter Kennern, doch nie eigentlich populär geworden, reich an Erfolgen und Katastrophen: sie ist eine der raren Erscheinungen, von denen man sagen kann, daß ihnen Genialität anhaftet ...

Ihre schriftstellerische Existenz rundet sich, 1951, durch die Buch-Sammlung ihrer bisher verstreuten Erzählungen unter dem Titel *The Ballad of the Sad Café* ... Die Titelgeschichte im Umfang eines kleinen Romans ist wohl das geschlossenste, künstlerischste und deprimierendste Stück Prosa, das die Autorin je geschrieben hat ...

Nahe dem „February House" in Brooklyn verlief die Sand Street mit ihren kleinen Bars. Dort pflegte die Autorin einzukehren, und dort traf sie einen merkwürdigen Buckligen, der die Gäste durch seine Verschrobenheit beeindruckte und von jedermann freigehalten wurde. Er gehörte zum Bestand dieser Café-Kneipen. Carson McCullers beobachtete ihn zwei Jahre lang, ehe ihre Intuition ihn umformte zum Vetter Lymon, dem Buckligen in der *Ballade vom traurigen Café*.

Alle Eigenheiten des Werks der McCullers sind in der *Ballade* zur Vollendung entwickelt. Es ist, als habe ihre Dichtung nunmehr die wahre Gestalt gefunden ...

Das tragische Dreiecksgeschehen zwischen Miss Amelia, dem Buckligen und dem Zuchthäusler Marvin Macy rührt an die elementaren Bedingungen der menschlichen Existenz. Es bedeutet die Umkehrung aller romantischen Liebesvorstellungen. Der Rollentausch zwischen Mann und Frau, immer schon ein Motiv der McCullers, ist mit skurrilen Mitteln gleichsam auf eine höhere Ebene der Realität transponiert. Im Grunde ist diese Geschichte eine Parabel auf die tragische Konzeption jeder außerordentlichen Natur.

(Dieter Lattmann, „Der Poet – ein einsamer Jäger. Die herben Märchen der Carson McCullers," *Über Carson McCullers,* hg. Gerd Haffmanns, Zürich: Diogenes, 1974, S. 99/100, 117/18.)

Few readers will insist that Mrs. McCullers' image of love should be touched by the Corneillian attributes of reasonableness and high-soulfulness – the age requires another image, less rational, perhaps, and more grotesque. But many readers will regret that no one in the novelette seems to have full access to his experience, to have any ultimate or even provisional understanding of it. In a sense, the work denies the possibility of *recognition* and avoids, therefore, the fictional equivalent of tragedy, a feature symptomatic of an age in which experience seems, more than ever, unyielding to human intelligence. Moreover, when love specifies the only contact between the hero and his world, heroism itself becomes not merely a call to isolation as in tragedy, but also an inducement to surrender all volition. Without volition no external field for interests or our actions can ever be defined. The wages of alienation are always compounded. Irony prevails. It is the envoy, the style of anonymous celebration and immitigable sadness, that raises the work to the condition of a haunting performance. The style of pretended ballad reticence and naïveté, of folk motifs and stark tragedy, of augurs and foreshadowing, of incremental repetition and telescoped action – the enfabled style seems to incarnate the very spirit of story-telling whose medium is language in and for itself...

(Ihab Hassan, *Radical Innocence. Studies in the Contemporary American Novel,* Princeton, New Jersey: © by Princeton University Press, 1961, pp. 226–27. Reprinted by permission.)

Out of the still and twisted world in which her imagination dwells, Mrs. McCullers has drawn some truths that come home to all men. She has illuminated the possibilities for loneliness and the capacities for deviant behavior that mark the human lot. But there is a troubling sense of something wanting in what she does. The world of the adolescent child is, after all, only a promise of life to come in adulthood. The crazy, private world of her freakish and tortured adults is on the periphery of our experience, even if a significantly disturbing one. It is a narrow corner of human existence that she has chosen to exploit in her fiction. Her view of man's fate, therefore, adds little, in the largest sense, to the dimensions of our understanding. The gothic view of life has conjured up the terror of life but has not weighed the consequences of that terror. Mrs. McCullers knows something of the conditions under which life must be carried on, but she has gone beyond this to examine how men might endure under these conditions. There is no room in her work for the *consequences* of human action; there is no sense of the continuity of life. She has succeeded perhaps too well in creating an art form that is cut off from life. It is a form cut off from society, from morality, from religion, from ideas, from concern with man's burden or with man's hope.

(Chester E. Eisinger, *Fiction of the Forties,* Chicago: University of Chicago Press, 1963, p. 258. Reprinted by permission.)

3. Writing in the New South

Certainly the post-World War II South offers little to allay the fears of the 1920s and '30s. The New South of commerce, speculation, and industrial growth has become a permanent reality. Of course no one would argue that the rapid development of the South in the 20th century has been without its advantages. Southern universities have prospered. And many of the negative legacies of the past, the oppressive poverty, the vicious share-cropping system, the rural isolation and illiteracy, the crimes of segregation, are gradually disappearing. But the necessary changes have brought their modern plagues, and no Southerner, no matter how enthusiastic he may be about progress and the new wealth, would deny that the face of his land has lost something of its old character.

The last few decades have brought more jobs and more money, but they have also brought the interstate, mass advertizing, commercial television, the shopping center, rampant tourism, and the general desolate urban-suburban sprawl. A modern Southern city begins to resemble anywhere and nowhere, a bleak uniformity of chain stores, parking lots, motels, pizza parlors, high-rise apartments, and the mobile home. This is, at least, the South most visitors would see, and the South that most Southerners confront daily when leaving their suburban neighborhoods on the way to work.

Certainly, outside the commercial centers, vestiges of the old South still persist. And if the farms are larger and less populous, the farmlands continue to flourish. Almost any back road in North Carolina or Mississippi will eventually lead past a rotting cabin, an abandoned mansion, and perhaps an old flop-eared mule; but it will also lead past country stores, well-kept white wooden churches, and small towns full of large porches. Southern evenings continue to come alive with the nervous ritual dance of fireflies and with the voluminous drone of crickets. And along the country roads, the Southern landscape, in all its variety and lushness and mystery, still overwhelms, still remains a supreme presence .

But the South has changed, perhaps more in the last thirty years than in its entire history, and it has changed toward the rest of the United States, toward a uniform existence of the same desires and the same tastes. Because of this, not a few Southern writers, even those who continue to write about the South, are left to rely on their memories . . .

If this is the case, how does one explain the continuing vitality of Southern literature, even in the present decade when the changes in the South toward a standardized America now seem beyond control? No literary tradition can survive merely because the times are ripe for satire. One good reason is that the South is still nourished by strong folk traditions, traditions that are preserved mainly through music and language. For if the visual community has changed, even disappeared, a certain communal identity remains alive, and it remains alive especially in the act of speech.

The first difference that strikes a visitor to the South is the language, the accents, the tones, the vocabulary, and the rhythms. It is an English as distinct as the English of Ireland. Unlike the stage Southern accent made popular by commercial television, the best of Southern speech is rooted in a rural, oral tradition where the expressive power of language is highly prized. Characterized by concrete, sensual detail, sly humor, and vivid, dramatic images, the folk speech of both black and white can attain a rich evocative beauty, as anyone who has listened to Mississippi John Hurt or Doc Watson can attest.

The South has always sustained a strong verbal awareness, with a conscious self-delight in creating new expressive forms. It is no accident that three of the most original forms of popular music in the 20th century, jazz, the blues, and bluegrass, had their beginnings in the South. The two dominant folk cultures of the South, the Negro and the Scotch-Irish, brought with them already richly developed oral traditions in which those with special gifts for expression were praised and publicly encouraged . . . The presence and creative force of these two cultures, their intermingling and mutual influence especially in the 20th century, may help explain the special skills the South demonstrates in the short story. (1977)

(Benjamin Forkner and Patrick Samway, "Introduction," *Stories of the Modern South,* New York: Bantam, 1978, pp. xiv-xvi.)

A Brief Guide to Literary Terms

Atmosphere: The mood pervading a literary work, arousing in the reader expectations as to the course of events, whether happy or disastrous. Atmosphere is transmitted through the description of setting and character.
Ballad: A narrative song-poem relating a unique dramatic event in a form suitable for singing. Folk ballads, with their traditional melodies, were transmitted orally, and most were constantly modified in the process. They are striking for their great compression, abrupt transitions, and dramatic contrasts. The form often makes use of conventional figures of speech and descriptive clichés, but the best ballads are vivid and concrete. Although they deal with strong passions, ballads are usually objective and impersonal and pay little attention to character analysis, setting, or moralizing. Their subjects are varied: domestic episodes, dying for love, murder, loyalty, riddles, outlawry, loss at sea, war, humour, fairy enchantment, the demon lover, supernatural visitations.
Characterization: The writer can introduce his persons either directly, telling the reader the person's qualities, or through action, showing the person's deeds and rendering his words and thoughts. Minor figures are frequently presented in only one aspect as "flat" characters. When persons are more fully shown they are called "round" characters. The main figures of a literary work of art are likely to be developing, dynamic characters.
Complications: Complexities, difficulties, confusions, crises in a prose narrative or a drama. See *Plot*.
Flashback: An interruption in the continuity of a story by the narration of some episode which took place earlier.
Foil: A character who, by contrast, sets off or helps define more clearly another character.
Foreshadowing: Hints of what is to come. Because of such advance hints or allusions we are not shocked by what happens, but rather we experience suspense as we wait for the expected to come about.
Metaphor: In a "simile" items from different classes are explicitly compared by a connective, such as "like," "as," or "than," or by a verb as "to seem," or "to appear": "Seems he a dove? His feathers are but borrowed." (Shakespeare). A metaphor asserts the identity of

terms that are literally incompatible without using connectives: "She is the rose, the glory of the day." (Spenser).

Motivation: The combination of circumstances and psychological foundation that makes plausible the actions of a character by supplying them with a reasonable basis.

Narrator: See *Point of view*.

Novelette: It is a form intermediate between the short story and the novel, having a greater scope than a short story but being shorter and less elaborate than a novel. It is designed to be read at a single sitting and to produce a single, concentrated effect.

Plot: The writer's arrangement of the happenings in a story or novel. It usually includes an exposition, a rising action, complications and crises, a climax (turning-point), a falling action, and a dénouement. These terms go back to Aristotelian dramatic theory.

Point of View: An author must choose a point of view (a perspective) from which he/she can narrate his/her story. There is a broad distinction between the participant and non-participant points of view. The first-person point of view means that there is a narrator ("I") who tells the story. A story told from the third-person point of view does not have a clearly recognizable narrator, however, often a hidden narrator can be felt who is then called an "implied" narrator. In *The Ballad of the Sad Café* the implied narrator (who at times might be identified with the author) plays a remarkably lively role insofar as he frequently steps out of the hidden role as "teller", commenting on the narrative process, evaluating the events he relates, or philosophizing. Although the teller of the tale never introduces himself as a character, he takes a recognizable stand on what he describes, thus subjecting himself to the reader's response and criticism.

Setting: The setting of a story is the locale and period in which its action takes place. Sometimes the setting is lightly sketched, presented only because the story has to take place somewhere and at some time. Often, however, the setting is important, giving us the feel of the people who move through it. It may also be symbolic.

Suspense: As a plot proceeds it arouses expectations in the reader as to future events, complications, crises. The uncertainty about what is going to happen, especially to characters we can identify with, is called suspense. It is an important element in the plot.

Symbol: A symbol is an object that is used to represent something abstract. Thus, a symbol is both itself and something else that it suggests, a kind of manifestation of something too complex or too elusive to be otherwise revealed. The café as the setting of this novel has a highly symbolic quality.

Theme: Usually a story is about a general topic, it has a meaning, a point – a theme. However, a story is not simply an illustration of a theme, but has a variety of details that modify any abstract statement. We can talk about the theme – what the story adds up to – as long as we do not think a statement of the theme is equivalent to or a substitution for the whole story.

Time-lapse technique: Originally a term used in the field of photography, then in drama and fiction. It means that the narrating time is much shorter than the acting time, i.e. the processes described take much longer than the time needed to relate them. It is also called compression. Its opposite is called slow-motion presentation or expansion.

Selected Bibliography

Carr, Virginia S. *The Lonely Hunter. A Biography of Carson McCullers.* Garden City, N.Y.: Anchor Press, 1976.

Eisinger, Chester E. *Fiction of the Forties.* Chicago: University of Chicago Press, 1963.

Evans, Oliver. *Carson McCullers. Her Life and Work.* London: Peter Owen, 1965.

Forkner, Benjamin and Patrick Samway. *Stories of the Modern South.* New York: Bantam, 1978.

Gaillard, Dawson F. "The Presence of the Narrator in Carson McCullers' The Ballad of the Sad Café," *Mississippi Quarterly,* 25 (1972) 419–27.

Hassan, Ihab. "Carson McCullers," *Radical Innocence: Studies in the Contemporary American Novel.* Princeton, N.J.: Princeton University Press, 1961, 205–29.

Hassan, Ihab. *Contemporary American Literature 1945–1972. An Introduction.* New York: Frederick Ungar Publishing Co., 1974.

Kazin, Alfred. *Bright Book of Life. American Novelists and Storytellers from Hemingway to Mailer.* Boston-Toronto: Little, Brown and Co., 1971.

Lattmann, Dieter. "Der Poet – ein einsamer Jäger. Die herben Märchen der Carson McCullers," *Über Carson McCullers.* Hg. Gerd Haffmanns, Zürich: Diogenes, 1974, 99–121.

McCullers, Carson. "The Flowering Dream," *The Mortgaged Heart.* Harmondsworth: Penguin, 1975, 280–87.

Millichap, Joseph R. "Carson McCullers' Literary Ballad," *The Georgia Review,* 27 (1973), 329–39.

Rubin, Louis D., Jr. *The Faraway Country. Writers of the Modern South.* Seattle: University of Washington Press, 1963.